How to ...

get ~~the most from your~~

COLES NOTES

Key Point

Basic concepts in point form.

Close Up

Additional hints, notes, tips or background information.

Watch Out!

Areas where problems frequently occur.

Quick Tip

Concise ideas to help you learn what you need to know.

Remember This!

Essential material for mastery of the topic.

Your Guide to ...

Public
Speaking

Formal speeches

Impromptu talks

Using microphones &

visual aids

COLES NOTES have been an indispensable aid to students on five continents since 1948.

COLES NOTES now offer titles on a wide range of general interest topics as well as traditional academic subject areas and individual literary works. All COLES NOTES are written by experts in their fields and reviewed for accuracy by independent authorities and the Coles Editorial Board.

COLES NOTES provide clear, concise explanations of their subject areas. Proper use of COLES NOTES will result in a broader understanding of the topic being studied. For academic subjects, Coles Notes are an invaluable aid for study, review and exam preparation. For literary works, COLES NOTES provide interesting interpretations and evaluations which supplement the text but are not intended as a substitute for reading the text itself. Use of the NOTES will serve not only to clarify the material being studied, but should enhance the reader's enjoyment of the topic.

© Copyright 1998 and Published by
COLES PUBLISHING. A division of Prospero Books
Toronto – Canada
Printed in Canada

Cataloguing in Publication Data

Your guide to—public speaking :
formal speeches, impromtu talks, using microphones & visual aids

(Coles notes) ISBN 0-7740-0582-3

1. Public speaking. I. Series.

PN4121.Y68 1998   808.5'1   C98-930470-1

Publisher: Nigel Berrisford
Editing: Paul Kropp Communications
Book design: Karen Petherick, Markham, Ontario
Layout: Richard Hunt

Manufactured by Webcom Limited
Cover finish: Webcom's Exclusive DURACOAT

Contents

CHAPTER ONE

Speaking in public: thinking ahead

"Our plans miscarry because we have no aim."
- Seneca

Day-to-day conversations are pretty relaxed. You chat about one thing, then switch to another without even thinking. But the minute you have to stand up and face an audience, speaking gets a lot more complicated.

For example, your boss informs you that you have to "sell" a dozen potential customers on a product you're developing. Or you feel strongly that your home and school meeting is being railroaded into spending too much money for the new adventure playground and someone needs to speak against it. Or you want to fight a proposed new mega-mall development which you feel will create traffic chaos in your neighborhood. So you're going to have to stand up in front of a sea of faces - not all of them friendly. No one will be giving you feedback - questions or comments - to keep your ideas flowing. You are the center of attention. All eyes and ears are on you. There will be no time to pause and sort out your ideas. You just have to do it - give a speech that will keep everyone enthralled for five, 10 or 40 minutes.

For most people, the thought of addressing an audience brings on instant panic. In fact, numerous surveys have shown that what many people fear most is not falling off a bridge or dying in a car crash, it's being asked to stand in front of a group and talk.

If that's how you feel, relax. Public speaking is easier than you think. A little planning, a little practice and you, too, can star in your own presentation.

Why bother to learn to speak in public? Solid public-speaking skills can certainly further career opportunities, but they also free you to express your opinion on the spur of the moment without fear of making a fool of yourself. Knowing that you can use spoken language effectively gives you the confidence to stand for president of your ratepayers' association, or toast the bride at your sister's wedding, or present to the boss that really innovative idea you've been mulling over.

How long does it take to become a good public speaker? That depends on how good you want to be and where you're starting. Some people are natural speakers, quite comfortable in front of groups, good at sounding confident. Once they've learned a few simple techniques for putting ideas together effectively, it might take them only two or three speaking opportunities to become excellent public speakers.

But don't despair. Even people who are not natural speakers can soon feel comfortable and confident once they've practiced some simple techniques. Flip through this book and you'll learn enough tricks of the talking trade that you'll feel as though you've been giving talks all your life.

PREPARATION MAKES A DIFFERENCE

What's so bad about just standing up and spouting off? Why bother to plan? Have you ever been in a situation similar to this one?

"Tell visitors at the local museum all about woodcarving? Sure, no problem. I've been doing it for 20 years. Right this minute? Here I come."

And in no time you're facing 40 interested people, you've got a chisel in one hand, a hunk of wood in the other and all that's coming out of your mouth is "Um ... er ... it's like ... what I mean is ... "

Everyone's staring at you, your mind has gone blank and it's too late to ask yourself, "What do I say first? Where do I go from here?"

The embarrassment of such moments can be avoided with 10 minutes of preparation. Given 20 minutes forewarning, you can sound like a pro. The secret is to have a plan in mind for pulling together and arranging the necessary information. All talks – from simple and spontaneous to complex and formal – fit one pattern. Anyone who knows the basic components can pull together an effective comment, rebuttal, announcement or talk in just a few minutes. But it can't be done without a certain amount of preparation. Someone once said about public speaking that people have a choice: you can panic before the talk or during the talk. If you channel your panic into preparation, you won't find yourself in trouble during the speech.

DECIDING ON THE TYPE OF SPEECH

Save yourself time and trouble from the start by defining the limitations of your talk. What you say and how you say it will largely be determined by the size and nature of the audience and by the type of room you'll be in. Think, first, about the audience you'll be facing. What are their needs and expectations? If they already know something about the subject of your talk (you're speaking to a peer group or professional colleagues, for example), they'll be looking for unusual insights. If they know nothing about the subject, they'll be looking for background information and context.

Think, also, about the size of your audience. A small group might feel comfortable with a chatty approach. For a large group, a more formal talk might work better. And what about the room? Is it so large that a microphone will be necessary? So small that you'll be very close to your audience? Will any nearby presentation create distracting noise? (This often happens at conferences where six or seven presentations are running simultaneously.) Is the room provided with audio-visual equipment such as an overhead projector, flipcharts or black/white boards? Knowing the physical components of the setting will help you begin to shape your speech.

Many decisions about your speech will be determined by the length of time you've been given. In a long speech (20 or 30 minutes) you have time to develop several points and illustrate them with lengthy anecdotes. In a five- or 10-minute speech you need to find a succinct way to make important points.

REASONS FOR SPEAKING

Speakers rise to their feet with one of four objectives: they want to inform, explain, convince or entertain. Although many speeches contain a little of all four, it's important to know the primary reason for the speech, where the real emphasis lies. What exactly are you trying to achieve? What do you want the audience to take home with them?

If your main goal is to inform your audience, then you need to build your talk around the journalist's six points. Tell them who, what, where, when, why and how. If you want to explain something, divide your topic into easily followed steps. To convince or persuade an audience, prepare arguments to show why something is or is not a good idea. To entertain, shape the material into a humorous story. Chances are you'll use all of these approaches in a long speech, but you need to know which is the overriding goal if you are to create an effective speech.

Survival tips for speakers

Part of being a good public speaker is know ing the right questions to ask when you're invited to give a talk. Always begin by asking for a specific topic. Beware the club president who says: "Anything you have to say will interest our members." Maybe, maybe not. Ask about the club activities and why you, in particular, were asked to speak. Throw out some possible topics you feel comfortable talking about. Don't agree to make a presentation until you feel sure your host understands and is happy with the topic you are proposing.

Also, beware taking on a topic that will entail enormous amounts of research. If you're asked to talk about the problems caused by the increased traffic flow in your neighborhood, and you can immediately think of three or four main points you want to make, this is probably a reasonable talk for you to prepare. But if you have no opinions, no background and don't care, think twice about accepting.

Having accepted, immediately ask some pertinent questions about arrangements that might affect your presentation:

1. How long are you expected to talk?
2. Where will you sit before and after your talk?
3. If you need audio-visual equipment, when can you set up and test it?
4. If you're not the only speaker, where will your talk fit into the program?
5. Will there be special guests in the audience you should be aware of?
6. Who is going to introduce you and how much background material is needed? (Be careful not to give information you will be using in your talk. You don't want the introducer stealing your thunder.)

CHAPTER TWO

Zeroing in on what you want to say

"The secret of being a bore is to tell everything."
-Voltaire

As a speaker, your most important job is to keep your listeners listening. If you ramble from one topic to another or try to present too much information about your subject, the audience will feel confused, annoyed and, ultimately, bored. Only a small amount of material can be covered effectively in the allotted 10, 20 or 40 minutes, so you have to find a way to zero in on the important aspects of your talk. Save yourself time and trouble by thinking this through before you start to write your speech.

One way to define and then refine your topic is by making lists. Perhaps you've been asked to explain the global consequences of acid rain to an audience with little background in the subject. This is a huge and complex topic about which you happen to know a great deal. You can't cram the knowledge you have acquired over 10 years in the field into one 20-minute talk. You have to pick and choose.

BRAINSTORMING

Begin with a session of brainstorming. Brainstorming is a term often associated with a group sitting around a table throwing out ideas to solve a particular problem. It's a way to liberate the mind from rigid, linear thinking and bring to the surface new and often startling approaches to a problem. This same technique can be used just as effectively by individuals.

Three major advantages of brainstorming are:

- a quick start. Rather than agonizing over where to begin a talk, you simply plunge in.
- an effective way to prime the pump. You'll find that ideas will flow faster and faster as you fill the page.
- more creative ideas. Brainstorming often results in ideas for topics or methods of organizing the material that are fresher and more exciting than any you'd get from straight logical thinking.

For many people, brainstorming imitates the way they naturally think – flashes of ideas, sudden images, unattached words. For others, it's a way to break out of rigid habits and let the subconscious – an anarchic and wildly creative area we too often suppress – do some of the hard work of thinking.

The one cardinal rule of brainstorming is this: don't censor. Every idea, notion, fragment goes down on paper. No one will see this. No one will scoff. An idea you thought of rejecting the second it appeared in your imagination might well be the very one that leads to a breakthrough in your approach.

HOW TO START

To brainstorm effectively you need to be in a relaxed state of mind in a quiet room with paper and pencil or computer handy. Focus on your topic. Visualizing aspects of it in concrete form is often a good way to start the process off. Remember, you aren't thinking, you're just reacting to the stimulus. Think about or visualize your topic, and then write as quickly as possible every image, word, phrase, number, name that comes to you. No complete sentences. Just fragments. No matter how far out, esoteric or seemingly irrelevant. You want lots of material to choose from later on.

Now, remove yourself from the situation for a while. You've just spent an intense half hour or more. Your brain needs to relax. So have lunch, make some calls, anything to give your mind some downtime. Once you distance yourself from that untrammeled outpouring, you'll be able to see how brilliant some of your "random wanderings" actually were (and tactfully ignore the really dumb ideas on your list).

To create list number two, hunt through your brainstormed ideas looking for words, names, phrases, fragments of ideas that seem to have some meaningful relationship with each other. Gather these together in groups. In brainstorming vocabulary, this is called "clustering." Your second list should be several (or many) groups of these clustered fragments.

For the next stage of organizing, you need to name your sections. Consider this as still part of the second list. Look at each grouping and ask yourself: What unites these ideas? How can I name this relationship?

What have you got so far? A jumble of ideas, gathered into groupings that have now been named. You are starting to organize the mass of possibilities for your speech into topics to create an outline. Now is the moment to remind yourself about your audience's needs and expectations. Have you missed out any topic essential to understanding your subject? Add it to the list. Does any topic on the list seem irrelevant for this audience or this particular talk? Circle it, put it to one side, but don't discard it yet. You never know what might be useful at a later stage of development.

By now you're well along the road to creating a workable outline for your talk. And instead of having to pare a huge subject down to a manageable length, brainstorming has allowed you to pull together only the segments of the subject likely to interest or inform your particular audience. You've pulled together the ideas that look most promising for this particular topic.

With list number three, you start to focus the topic more specifically. Can you see a direction beginning to emerge, a section of your larger subject that would be most likely to interest or inform the particular audience you'll be addressing? Remember, you can't tell the audience everything. You're looking for a way to narrow the subject, focus it to fit the time allotted and the interests of the audience.

As a direction or slant begins to emerge from the original jumble of possibilities in your first list, you may need to continue with a fourth and fifth list to streamline your subject. Or you may prefer to stay with a broader look at the topic with the idea of weeding out unneeded sections at a later stage. But list by list, you've come closer to a manageable focus on your subject. There will be more refining and focusing, but you now have a rough shape for your talk and probably some key questions to ask as you research specific material.

The outline

Arrange your brainstorming ideas into
a skeleton outline.
(We'll expand on this later.)

Introduction

Main Idea 1
- backup
- backup

Main Idea 2
- backup
- backup

Main Idea 3
- backup
- backup

Main Idea 4
- backup
- backup

Summary

Closing Sentence

CHAPTER THREE

Researching

"The most immutable barrier in nature is
between one man's thoughts and another's."
– *William James*

Most speeches require some researching. Even if you know
your topic cold, chances are you'll need to check a reference, look
up a quote to get the exact wording, or catch up with the latest
findings in your field. Often you're after a hard-to-find fact, so
knowing how to effectively tackle research can save you time and
effort later – and perhaps embarrassment during the Q & A period
after your talk.

USING THE LIBRARY

The local library is an invaluable resource for any topic you're
researching, but if libraries are unknown territory for you, here are
a few tips:

- Ask reference librarians for help. That's what they're paid to
  do.

- Most libraries have computerized indexes. Use the "key word"
  option for a broad search of your subject. Try several synonyms
  of your key word to get the best coverage.

- Most libraries use the Dewey decimal system to organize material. Broad subject headings are posted on the ends of book
  stacks. For example, science is labeled 500. Then the subject
  is subdivided. Botany is 580. Physics is 530. Most libraries post

signs guiding you to the larger subjects. This gets you to the right section of the library quickly. You can ask librarians to find a book for you. They may frown, but they're wonderfully efficient.

- When you find a useful book, look at the books on either side of it. Other valuable resources may be sitting right there beside the book you found in the catalogue.

- When consulting a book, use the table of contents (at the front) and the index (at the back) to discover whether the book contains information you're after and where to find it quickly. You seldom need to read the whole book.

- Record the book title and page number for your researched information immediately following the information. Then, if you need to check facts or add more information, you'll be able to find the reference quickly.

- Use the vertical files. Libraries clip magazine and newspaper articles of current information that has not yet made it into books. This is a valuable source of up-to-the-minute information on your topic.

- Use the periodical index. Many libraries have computer access to current periodicals that will give you current information about your subject.

- Use the Internet. For an effective search, use a number of synonyms for your key words, then print out the useful Web sites.

- Use *Bartlett's Familiar Quotations* and *The Oxford Dictionary of Quotations*. Check the indexes for your key words. Someone famous may have made a pithy remark that will dress up your talk.

- Look through joke and anecdote books, then personalize the information to fit your speech.

INTERVIEW EXPERTS

Most people are willing if not eager to talk about subjects they know well. Both phone and in-person interviews can be quick ways to gather hard-to-find information, but you must prepare ahead so that you don't irritate your sources by wasting time. Follow these guidelines:

1. Beforehand, make a list of questions. Keep them short and to the point.

2. Introduce yourself and succinctly give your reason for calling. If you think you'll stammer and backtrack, write out exactly what you want to say. Sounding professional can make the difference between an expert willing to talk to you and someone who brushes you off as a nuisance.

3. During the conversation, take brief notes to remind yourself of what was said. It's embarrassing to you and annoying to the expert if you have to phone back to get exact figures or check spelling. Taping a face-to-face interview is useful as long as you don't have to interrupt the flow of conversation to fool with the equipment. A small tape-recorder with good microphone pick-up can be placed unobtrusively on the floor or a nearby table so your interview subject isn't distracted by it. Before you arrive, be sure to check your batteries and make yourself familiar with the buttons so you can set the tape-recorder up at the beginning of the interview with little fuss. In winter, be sure to keep the batteries warm so they'll be ready to work when you need them. Use 90-minute tapes to minimize flipping and changing.

Try to make your interview as short as possible to avoid wasting your expert's valuable time. He or she will be more willing to answer quick questions that may come up later in the writing process if you've been businesslike during the interview. At the end of the interview, always ask if the expert would like to add anything. This way you can be sure you've covered every aspect of the subject. As soon as you put the phone down or are back in your car, add any remembered details to your notes. If you wait, they'll disappear from your memory.

Tools of the trade

For effective researching you'll need:

- file cards or a notebook
- several pens or pencils
- money for photocopies and Internet access

Also useful:

- tape-recorder
- camera

INTERVIEW YOURSELF

Your feelings and experiences are valid material for talks. Personal anecdotes that illuminate points you are making can brighten up a speech and keep listeners interested. Search your memory for incidents that can add a personal dimension to your speech. If you can also inject some humor this way, so much the better.

Suppose you are giving a talk on the ownership and care of big dogs – Great Danes, for example. One of the major points you'll be emphasizing is the dog's need for exercise – every day, rain or shine, 365 days a year. You can underline this humorously with an anecdote like the following: "Several years ago my neighbor made a big mistake – he bought a Great Dane as a pet for his teenage daughter. Two years later she went off to university and guess who had to walk the dog? My neighbor is 5′ 3″ and weighs, after a good meal, about 120 pounds. The dog outweighs him by at least 30 pounds and stands as high as his shoulder. Whenever I see him being towed down the street, I wonder: Is he walking the dog or is the dog walking him? A point to consider when you're thinking of buying a pet."

KEEPING TRACK

You may have researched some fascinating material but how are you going to retrieve information that will back up the points you want to make? You need an organized method for collecting information. Many people find 3 x 5 inch or 4 x 6 inch file cards an efficient way to keep track of the facts they turn up. Since your list making has pinpointed questions that need answers, one way to keep information sorted is to write the questions at the top of file cards or notebook pages and jot the information under the question as your research turns up the answer. Be sure to keep track of the source of each piece of information by noting down the book title and page number or magazine article and issue number. Otherwise it can take hours to relocate a quote that turns out to be key to an argument but must be correctly attributed.

Whether you use questions or simply key words to label your file cards, a logical way of organizing the mass of material you are collecting is essential to efficient retrieval later on.

CHAPTER FOUR

Organizing your material

Your initial lists have given you a skeleton outline for your speech, and your research has provided content. Now you have to decide how you're going to use all this material. Each card is neatly labeled and you probably have five or six with partial answers for each question or key word you've used. Although not all of this material will prove useful, most of it will. Some will even suggest interesting directions you may not have considered earlier. So now you have to sift and sort to find what will be useful and what can be discarded.

This initial sifting and sorting is actually your first attempt to organize your speech, so it helps to know what kinds of material you're looking for. Keep in mind that every speech has three parts: beginning, middle, end. Each of these sections has an important role to play in the overall impact of your presentation. The beginning must grab your listeners' attention and at the same time give them a quick overview of the material you are going to cover. The middle is the meat of the talk and will take 80 percent of your time. Here you need facts, figures and anecdotes to back up the points you are making. The ending not only sums up the main thrust of the points you've been making, it should leave the audience with a challenge of some kind.

How do you decide what facts might make a good beginning and ending? Journalists writing for magazines have a handy guideline for this. They tend to open with their best quote, most startling fact or most telling anecdote. They close the piece with their second best. If you keep that thought tucked at the back of your mind

15

as you sift through your material, the right opening or closing remark often jumps out at you.

SIFTING YOUR RESEARCH

Once it's time to sort through your researched material, the value of having individual cards for each piece of information becomes obvious. It allows you to simply go through and make an initial rough sort. You'll end up with four piles:

1. Unusual or startling facts and quotes that might make a good opening.
2. The great mass of material that will back up the points you are going to make in the middle.
3. Good closing quotes or anecdotes.
4. The inevitable bits of information that no longer fit the speech that is taking shape.

However, don't discard pile four yet. You never know what might prove important at a later stage in the development of your talk.

The quick sort

- Sort your research cards into four piles: necessary information, possible opening/closing, interesting quotes or anecdotes, what you no longer need.
- Choose your main points from the "necessary" pile.
- Create idea cards using one point per card.
- Arrange your idea cards into a logical sequence.

CHOOSING THE FINAL ARRANGEMENT

Before you try organizing your material into a formal outline, stop for a moment and remind yourself of your reasons for giving this talk: to inform? explain? persuade? entertain? Most talks have an element of all four purposes, but talks tend to divide into two main groups: those which inform and those which persuade. Before you create the final outline for your talk, you need to be *clear* which of these purposes is paramount.

If you need to *persuade* your audience of your point of view, then your talk should build progressively toward your most important, most telling point. Talks that have a strong persuasive element need this build-up to a climax in order to be effective. For an example of a persuasive talk, see the sample speech in the appendix.

If your intent is simply to *inform*, you need a structure that allows you to get facts across clearly. A good plan for this type of talk is to begin with known information or the simplest concept, then move through a logical progression to the unknown or more difficult ideas.

Now that you've reminded yourself of your purpose, you can evaluate the information you've collected and decide where it would be most effective.

To get a feeling for the possible flow of your talk, take the cards in pile two (the middle or meat of your talk) and spread them out on the table. Here a journalist's trick can help you again. Look for the material that would make good starting and ending points. Once you have those, you'll often find that the rest of the material is easily organized into a logical flow from one idea or point to the next.

Just by organizing cards on the table you've created the skeleton outline of your talk. The questions or key words that grew out of your brainstorming session created sections for your talk, your research gave you content to explain and back up those ideas. But your outline still needs some refining. Now that you can see the structure of your talk, ask yourself what's missing or what has now become redundant.

A sample outline

The outline for a talk meant to explain the process of producing sugar from cane to finished product might look like this:

Introduction
1. Sugar is one of our most commonly used foods. We all have a bit of a sweet tooth.
2. How does sugar get from field to table?

Body
1. Extract juices from the cane.
   - a) detail
   - b) detail
2. Purify the raw juice.
   - a) detail
   - b) detail
3. Evaporate water from the juice.
   - a) detail
   - b) detail
4. Crystallize solid sugar from syrup.
   - a) detail
   - b) detail
5. Ordinary granulated table sugar comes from refined crystals.
   - a) detail
   - b) detail

Conclusion
1. Summary of steps

Outlining the how-to talk

So far we've talked about speeches that need facts in the form of researched material to support them. But you may be giving a talk about a subject where you are the expert. Let's take the example of a carver who suddenly found himself trying to explain how to carve – an activity he'd been engaged in for 20 years. For this kind of talk, the information on the file cards comes from sitting down and thinking through exactly how you do whatever it is that you are expert at. A plan for this type of speech could be laid out as a flow chart.

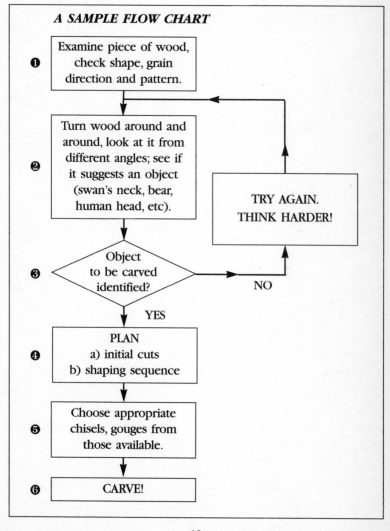

A SAMPLE FLOW CHART

❶ Examine piece of wood, check shape, grain direction and pattern.

❷ Turn wood around and around, look at it from different angles; see if it suggests an object (swan's neck, bear, human head, etc).

❸ Object to be carved identified?

NO

TRY AGAIN. THINK HARDER!

YES

❹ PLAN
a) initial cuts
b) shaping sequence

❺ Choose appropriate chisels, gouges from those available.

❻ CARVE!

Use brainstorming to help you organize the instant speech. If you have information or opinions about the subject under discussion, brainstorming techniques allow you to organize quickly and effectively for an answer, explanation or rebuttal.

CHAPTER FIVE

Writing out your talk

"Mind your speech a little lest you should mar your fortunes."
– Shakespeare

Brainstorming gave you main points for your talk, research has given you backup material, organizing has created an outline; now you need to write out your talk. Even though you will not be reading the speech or even memorizing it, you need to turn your ideas into sentences that flow logically from beginning to end. Just as sculptors shape their creation in a series of steps from the first rough outline crayoned on the stone to the smooth and polished finished statue, so you have to refine and refine your talk until the ideas flow effortlessly from one to the next.

SHAPING THE MATERIAL

A well-shaped talk has three parts:

1. Beginning (10 percent of time)
2. Middle (80 percent of time)
3. End (10 percent of time)

How do these parts of your talk help you "clue in" your audience? Let's look at some details.

Beginning

Your beginning (or introduction) must grab your listeners' attention and, at the same time, tell them what you're going to talk about. You could start off with the direct approach: "Today I'm going to tell you about blah ... blah ... blah ..." They'll know what you're going to talk to them about, but will they care? Probably not. Anyone who's been part of an audience knows how easy it is to tune out the speaker. To stop that from happening, you need the kind of "grabber" or "hook" that good journalists use to open a column. You want an opening that wakes up your listeners and puts them on the edge of their seats, while it hints at all the gems of wisdom to come.

How do you do that? When you were making your outline, you set aside some possibilities from your research – unusual, startling or funny information that might work as an opening. Have another look at this material to see what now seems most suited to the type of speech you want to make. Then work it into your opening in one of the following forms:

A question

"What is it that flies through the air, is shaped like a tiny hamburger, and goes *splat!* when it hits the ground? If you're thinking "a raindrop," you're right. And today I'm going to tell you how that tiny raindrop can destroy our world. It's actually a time bomb dropping on us, and its real name is … acid rain."

An anecdote

"One day, two hunters high in the Rocky Mountains came across a trail of giant footprints. Excited, they followed the tracks higher and higher into the mountains. Suddenly, ahead, they caught a glimpse of something moving. Although it was partially obscured by rocks and trees, it appeared very tall, with a human shape and covered with long hair. Was it the legendary Sasquatch? Or had the rarified air at this altitude clouded their judgment? Were their imaginations working overtime?"

A surprising, startling or disturbing fact

"Scientists tell us that because of the way we've mistreated our planet, the earth is getting warmer, and this "global warming" will cause dire problems in the future. Unless we find ways to stop or even reverse it, our days are numbered. For the next half hour we're going to look at the causes for this warming, then see if there is something those of us sitting in this room can do to stop it."

These examples show three ways to set up a "hook" or "grabber" that leads into a sentence or two describing what you propose to do in the remainder of the talk. Remember to keep the introduction short. Ten percent of your total time is plenty. All you're doing here is getting the audience ready to listen to what you have to say.

 Don't overwhelm your audience with too much, too fast. You can't fit every last researched detail into your talk. Be selective.

Middle

The middle (or body) is the bulk of your talk, 80 percent of your material, and the place where you are going to make your most telling arguments. First, remind yourself about your primary aim: Are you trying to inform, explain, persuade or entertain? In your outline you've already made a choice of direction, either building toward a crescendo if you're trying to persuade, or starting with the known and proceeding toward the unknown if you're primarily informing. Now you need to turn the points in your outline into a seamless, flowing narrative that will effectively accomplish your aim.

Remember, also, as you start to put the middle together, that an audience of listeners cannot take in and make sense of as much information as an audience of readers. Where a pamphlet or newsletter article can present many points, a speaker can effectively get across only three or four. What you're trying to do, as you write out your talk, is not cover everything that could be said but to give your talk *ear appeal*.

Begin by reading through your outline. You've organized your points in a logical sequence and you've made notes about the backup facts and figures that will prove your points. Do you have too much backup? Will all the facts just become oral clutter? Underline the two or three most effective details for each point, the ones you must include, and keep the others in reserve in case they're needed.

As you start to write, you'll want to have in your mind a number of techniques for getting your points across effectively. These are:

1. Vary your presentation to keep your listeners interested.
2. Use transitional phrases to help them follow your line of thought.
3. Define your terms.
4. Make your sentences strong and direct.

Vary your presentation

Each point you make needs to be backed up. You need the authority of facts and figures if your audience is going to be convinced by your arguments or understand your explanation, but the way you present the facts and figures doesn't have to be as dry as dust. Add some variety to your presentation with a judicious use of examples, anecdotes and comparisons.

Examples Try to choose examples that tie into your audience's interests or background. If you are addressing the parents' group at your local school, use examples that involve schools and children. If you're addressing a group of geologists, draw your examples from interesting rock formations in the local area and their effect on land use and settlement patterns. Lead-in phrases, such as "for instance," "for example," "you'll recall" and "once upon a time," make listeners sit up and pay attention.

To make your examples immediate and compelling, use details that answer: who, where, when, what, how and why. And make the examples as particular to your audience as possible. Rather than saying "many people," bring the danger right home to them by saying "one-third of the people in this room" or "the person to your right or left." Examples force you to express your ideas in concrete rather than abstract terms.

Anecdotes Stories that illuminate or enlarge on the points you're making not only give an audience a welcome respite from facts and figures, they are also easier to remember. Keep anecdotes short and to the point, however. A story should enhance, not dominate, your talk. And if an anecdote comes out of your personal experience or the experience of someone connected to your audience, that makes it even more powerful.

Comparisons Your information is much more meaningful to an audience if they have a sense of how big, how far away, how heavy some important object is. Be sure to choose comparisons that are readily comprehensible. Abstract words like "gigantic" or "tiny" add nothing to a listener's understanding. Look for concrete details that create a picture in the listener's imagination, for example: "Gold is surprisingly heavy. One ounce is about the size of a sugar cube."

If you want to give the audience a feeling for something big and complex like an institution or project, pick one or two cogent comparisons. Don't try to cover every facet. You can't and the audience doesn't want to hear it.

Where will you find examples, anecdotes and comparisons? As well as looking through your researched material, your personal experiences may be a good source particularly for anecdotes. If humor is appropriate to the type of presentation and the type of audience, this is a good way to work it into your talk.

Useful source material

And I Quote: the Definitive Collection of Quotes, Sayings and Jokes for the Contemporary Speechmaker, by Ashton Applewhite, William R. Evans III and Andrew Fotheringham, St. Martin's Press, 1992.

Bartlett's Familiar Quotations, Little, Brown, 1980.

Executive's Treasury of Humour for Every Occasion, by W.R. Gerler, Parker Publishing, 1965.

The Public Speaker's Treasure Chest, by H.V. Prochnow and H.V. Prochnow Jr., Harper & Row, 1986.

Transitions and connections

It's important to remember that the human brain and ear don't work together as efficiently as the brain and eye. Readers can move at their own pace, go back to pick up a missed point or read the whole piece over again. Listeners get *one chance* at the material. If they don't hear or don't comprehend your point, they may lose the thread of the whole talk, and your efforts are wasted. So make it easy for them. Signal a change of direction, introduction of a new piece of information or a digression with transitional phrases. For example:

- Alert the audience that you are about to move from your introduction into the main body of your speech with such phrases as "My first point…;" "First let me explain…;" "Let's look first at…." These transitional phrases give your listeners time to prepare themselves to listen attentively.

- Help your listeners keep track of where you are by numbering your points: "In the second place…;" A third point…;" "Finally…;" "I'd like to end with…."

- If you need to interpolate, tell them you're going off on a tangent with such phrases as "To digress for a moment…;" "An interesting sidelight on this is…." Audiences need time to refocus when you're heading off on a new tack. Transitional phrases give them both the clue that a change is coming up and the opportunity to follow along easily.

- Repeat key points for emphasis. Your listeners can't go back and check on a point the way readers can, so repetition is a useful way to help them keep track of your argument.

Defining your terms

Words seldom mean exactly the same thing to everyone in a room. Even colleagues don't always agree on the nuances of professional terms, so it's always a good idea to define any term that may cause confusion or misunderstanding. Usually a clear definition of how you will be using any specialized term, presented near the beginning of your talk, will suffice. But if you'll be using several terms that might be unfamiliar to the majority of your audience – in a talk,

for example, arguing for closing down the local nuclear power plant –
you may want to list the words on a flip chart and remind your audience of their meanings as you use them.

Sentence variety

The most exciting subject can be made boring by a tedious
presentation. You can add a surprising amount of sparkle to your
talk simply by varying the types and lengths of sentences.

- Ask a question, then answer it. For example, "What cancer-caus-
  ing ingredient is most easily eliminated from your diet? Fat."

- Use a long sentence followed by a short one to add impact to
  a point you are making. "In 1859, an English naturalist published a treatise that would set in motion an ongoing, often
  acrimonious, debate between scientists and theologians the
  world over. His name? Charles Darwin."

- Turn some of your sentences around. Instead of: "Fat is the
  major enemy of a healthy lifestyle," try: "The major enemy of a
  healthy lifestyle is – fat!"

- Add punch to your delivery by deleting prepositions and con-
  nector phrases. Instead of: "He set about changing her looks,
  and by so doing he managed to change her life", try: "By changing her looks, he changed her life." Simple, short sentences can
  add energy and drama to your talk.

By keeping your vocabulary simple, your sentences tight and
energetic and your tone conversational, you are showing that you
care about your audience. The easier you make it for them, the more
appreciative they'll be towards you.

End

You've come to the end of your presentation. All your points
have been made and backed up and your audience is still awake and
listening intently. Don't sit down yet! Audiences need to be prepared
to stop listening. Not only must you give a clear signal that you're
coming to the end, you also want to take this last and possibly most
powerful opportunity to motivate your listeners to go out and make
use of the information you've presented.

An effective ending needs two components. First, a quick summary of your main points. Don't recapitulate your entire speech. Simply state, as briefly as possible, your main points. Use phrases that make it obvious you are summing up, for example: "And we can see that by doing this, this, this and this, we will...." Or you can reduce your main points to their simplest: "The four words to remember are this, this, this and this." A quick summing up will bring your speech into sharp focus and alert the audience that you are nearly finished.

Secondly, for a good ending, have a good exit line. Your closing line can do one of four things:

1. Simply tie back to your opening remarks. ("As I said at the start ...")

2. Predict the future. ("If we continue to pollute our lakes and streams, by the year 2010 your children and grandchildren will have no water to drink.")

3. Appeal to the emotions. ("Remember, every third person in this room will be affected adversely by second-hand smoke.")

4. Be a call to action. ("Finally, I urge all of you to donate time and money to your local conservation authority. Your children and grandchildren will thank you as they enjoy an unpolluted wilderness area.")

Remember:

- The key to clarity is organization.

- The key to organization is clear, logical thinking.

- The key to dynamic speaking is transforming clear, logical thinking into a message with impact, then delivering it in a compelling, vital and animated way.

CUTTING BACK AND TIMING

Suppose you've got your talk written out so each section flows seamlessly into the next. You've balanced light and heavy moments, facts and figures against anecdotes and examples but – it's way too long! Does it matter if your speech takes 50 rather than the 40 minutes you were asked for? Yes, it does. Time matters for a number of reasons but the most important is the audience's patience.

An audience that's been told a talk will last a certain amount of time has a built-in clock. Once you run over they start shifting in their seats, looking at watches – letting their attention wander. It's better to leave an audience craving more than wishing for less.

Time check

As a rough guideline to how close your talk is to your budgeted time and how well-balanced your points are, read it out loud into a tape-recorder and check it against this timeline:

> 2 minutes for introduction
>
> + 2 minutes for each main point
>
> + 2 minutes for each backup point under a main point
>
> + 2 minutes for each example
>
> + 2 minutes for the ending or summary
>
> = total minutes

The length of time your taped practice presentation took may or may not be the time a presentation in front of an audience will take. If you are comfortable in front of an audience, your taped time is probably accurate. If you're a beginner and know you speak more quickly when you're nervous, subtract about 5 percent from your taped time. If being nervous makes you speak slowly, add 5 percent. Now you have a clearer sense of the real time your talk will take.

If you're over your time limit, look for places where you can make cuts. Check to see if any sections are swollen out of proportion to the rest of the talk. This is always the first place to cut back. Or you might be giving too much supporting material for each point. Which of your examples, anecdotes or statistics are most effective? Which ones can be dropped? Another possibility is that you have too many main points. Can one be dropped entirely? And remember - none of this material is wasted. Keep it in reserve for the Q & A session that often follows a talk.

A listening audience can take in and retain much less material than a reading audience, so keep your presentation simple, direct and to the point. The easier you make it for your audience, the more receptive they will be - and the more effective you will be.

 ## Quick plan for drafting a talk

1. Decide on one or more primary goals.

2. List main points you wish to convey.

3. Beside each point, list arguments, supporting facts, examples, anecdotes to back it up.

4. Think of themes that connect these points. Put these in the introductory remarks.

5. Create a list of transitional phrases and insert them where they belong.

6. Check the pacing. Have you used lighter moments to balance emotionally tense or factually heavy sections?

7. List concluding points: a summary of arguments or a plan of action you want the audience to take away with them.

8. Prepare extra material as backup for the question and answer session.

PREPARING FOR THE Q & A SESSION

If your talk has been aimed at persuading or informing your audience, chances are it will generate questions. Preparing for the Q & A session is part of preparing for your talk. Any comment or query might be flung your way. How are you going to handle it? Just as important, when will the Q & A session happen? To keep your presentation on track, you need to be in charge of both how and when.

First, be prepared. Once you've organized your speech, sit down for another brainstorming session with yourself. Make a list of all the possible questions, quibbles and sidetracks your audience might throw at you. You need to second-guess your audience here. If you've been trying to persuade them to your point of view, what are the opposing points of view and how can they be countered? If you've been primarily explaining or informing, how much more do you know about the subject in case someone asks for extra details about one aspect or another?

Once you have a sense of the possible questions, make a list of the background facts and figures you'll need to have at the front of your mind in order to answer or refute any point made from the floor. If this information is too detailed to memorize, write it out so you can have the material at hand for quick reference.

If you're caught completely off-guard by a tricky question, be prepared to say: "That's an interesting point. I don't know the answer. Can anyone here help us with this?" Waffling and hedging will destroy the credibility you've already built with your talk. No one can be expected to know everything. If you can't answer a question, say so and, if possible, also say why – even if it's merely a statement such as, "That goes into an area beyond my expertise."

There will always be questions you don't *want* to answer. The most challenging is a question that requires much explanation and is of no interest to anyone in the room but the asker. One solution is to suggest the questioner speak to you privately after the formal part of the event is over.

Another problem is a question so rambling and incoherent that you don't know where to begin. Before you try to answer, restate the question so that it has some relevance to your topic. Try to do this in a helpful, rather than a put-down way. A comment such as

"I'm not sure I understand. Do you mean…?" will save face all around and gain you audience approval.

Next comes the question of when to take questions. Every so often you'll run into audience members who want to interrupt and ask questions during the talk. Decide beforehand if your nerves can stand the interruption; and if your talk will be fragmented and lose its impact if you stop to answer questions en route. Some presentations, like seminars with small groups being guided by a leader through a particular topic, lend themselves to this kind of audience participation. But if you're building toward a climax, or know you will answer most questions at some point in your talk, you may not want to be interrupted. Say so right at the beginning: "This topic always generates healthy discussion but I'd like to leave questions to the end when you have all the facts before you." And if an audience member persists in interrupting you, repeat the injunction: "I think you'll find that this will become clear a bit further on. I'll be glad to take questions at the end."

Think of the Q & A period as an add-on to the talk, not the ending. Questions are a weak way to end your presentation. Come to your conclusion by giving a summary of your points or issuing your call to action, say thank you, sit down and allow the audience to applaud for a minute or two while the impact of your talk sinks in, then stand and offer to take questions.

Another possibility, in an informal situation, especially if you've been informing or explaining, is to take questions at the end of the middle section when you've presented the bulk of the material. After five minutes, or when the questions seem to be falling off, you should pull the group back to the sense of being listeners. Use a comment like: "Your questions have rounded out the subject for us nicely, so let's summarize the conclusions we've come to. First…;" or whatever type of conclusion works best for your particular presentation.

The important point here is – don't let the Q & A session spoil the effect your well-prepared talk has made. Take charge and integrate it into the flow of the presentation. Then your audience will go away feeling both satisfied by and appreciative of your talk.

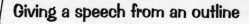

Giving a speech from an outline

Some people feel a speech loses the feeling of spontaneity if it is written out sentence by sentence and then reduced to notes. They prefer to deliver the speech straight from their outline. Don't be fooled by the word "spontaneous," however. No matter how "off-the-cuff" a speech may sound to the audience, it still must be carefully crafted. Your outline can range all the way from just main headings to detailed notes, but to get effective support and guidance from them, you must organize the material carefully. Here are some points to remember:

- Organize your points in logical order.
- Familiarize yourself thoroughly with your topic, so you know how the ideas process in sequence through your speech.
- Memorize your opening sentence so you start off confidently.
- Memorize your closing sentence, so you are certain to finish strongly.
- Make sure you can segue appropriately and effectively from one idea into the next.
- Practice giving your speech from your notes until your delivery is smooth, and you can say what you want to say effectively in the time allotted.

CHAPTER SIX

Adding pizzazz with audio-visual material

"It's all in the presentation."
- *Julia Child*

Why do people often use audio-visual (AV) aids (charts, slides, audio and video tapes) when giving a speech? Simply put, it's because such aids, intelligently chosen and expertly used, can help to:

- pep up your talk
- illustrate points you're making
- summarize what you've said so far
- give variety to your presentation methods (to stave off audience boredom)

The old saying reminds us, "One [well-chosen!] picture is worth a thousand words." These days, that includes revealing sound bites and videotape clips. Current technology makes it possible for speakers to use many different kinds of visuals and sound effects to add interest to a speech or presentation.

There are many of these audio-visual aids on the market today, with more coming every month. Let's take a look at what's available. Remember, you have to choose carefully which of those available to you will fit into your talk best and help you to tell your story as compellingly as possible.

WHAT TO CHOOSE?

AV aids are usually classified into the following three general categories:

1. Basic (low-tech)

*   storyboards, sketches – mounted, e.g., on foam board
    - hand-held, or on an easel
*   flip charts - prepared beforehand
    - write on
*   blackboards and chalk/white boards and markers
*   overhead projector and transparencies
    - prepared beforehand
    - write on
*   single slide projector (35 mm)

These basic aids, except for the last, are always used with a "live" commentary by the speaker. The slide projector is sometimes rigged with an accompanying tape-recorder and pre-recorded tape, providing a taped commentary and changing the slides automatically at the appropriate times.

2. Intermediate (medium-tech)

*   taped audio segments (speech excerpts, commentary, appropriate music, sound effects, etc.)
*   videotape clips (VCR and monitor)

3. Advanced (high-tech)

*   multi-slide projector (carousel or similar, two or more projectors with switcher/fader and remote control, to allow dissolves)
*   computer-generated overheads with special overhead projector (e.g., PowerPoint™ or similar) and a computer to produce the images

To go with the AV aids noted above, you will need some accessories:

*   suitable markers to write on visuals. These allow you to write essential information on blank visual displays, or supplementary comments on prepared displays.

- erasers for markers to get rid of comments or sketches that would distract from your presentation [with a flip-chart, you simply flip to your next point, or to a blank sheet you've placed next for the purpose.
- A suitable pointer – conventional or laser. This extends your reach so that you can point to selected features on your visual, without blocking them from your audience's view. The good-quality laser pointer, although expensive, is useful up to 30 feet (about 9 m), making it extremely useful on large projected visuals, where the screen is placed well out of normal human reach.

Visual aids are particularly useful in helping the audience keep track of statistics or vocabulary specific to your subject. But too many can be confusing. Choose the one that best suits the information you need to present from these six basic types.

1. Graphic and statistical diagrams
- picture graphs
- bar graphs
- line graphs
- pie charts

2. Graphic organizers
- hierarchical diagrams (a.k.a. organizational charts, which show "pecking order," top to bottom)
- relational diagrams, which show how two quantities (e.g., price of oranges and percentage of crop killed by freezing) are related, year by year

3. Charts and tables
- checklists
- mileage charts

4. Time displays
- timelines
- clocks
- calendars
- seasonal charts

5. Process diagrams

- sequential diagrams (a.k.a. flow charts)

6. Representational (pictorial) diagrams

- symbols
- maps
- line illustrations (drawings)
- photographs

SIMPLEST AND LEAST IS BEST

With so many types and subtypes to choose from, your choice of the most effective means for illustrating a desired point is often difficult, especially if the necessary information is available to you in several of the forms noted above. If you have to make your own visuals, or choose among several that are available pre-made, remember that the simplest, least cluttered, most easily seen will be your best choice. Above all, make sure that you don't put a visual into your talk just because it's available. A visual must clarify or effectively illustrate a point you couldn't make nearly as well without it. If it doesn't, it will divert your listeners' attention from the idea you're trying to present, thus hindering rather than helping you get your point across.

Your first priority should be to use the basic or low-tech aids as much as possible. Why? The reason is simple: they're the least likely to malfunction when you use them. They are also the easiest to operate, especially when you're under stress. If you can easily make use of medium or high-tech aids, and they will *significantly* enhance your presentation, by all means use them. *But be sure you know how to operate them, and be sure you've practiced until you know you can operate them reliably!* Generally, these more sophisticated aids require a lot more practice time for you to get proficient and confident in their operation. You should consider very carefully whether they really add enough to your presentation to warrant using them. And you need a backup plan if the high-tech equipment fails.

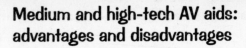

Medium and high-tech AV aids: advantages and disadvantages

These more sophisticated aids can enhance *some* presentations sufficiently to overcome their drawbacks *if you're prepared to live with a certain amount of unreliability!*

Taped audio and video segments can pep up a talk, as long as they are appropriate to vividly illustrate the point you're trying to make, the equipment involved doesn't break down and you can operate the equipment smoothly, without hesitating or fumbling.

A multi-projector arrangement with switcher/fader and remote control (for fades and dissolves) can give you spectacular visual effects, but the preparation time beforehand often makes its use unfeasible unless this is a presentation you're going to give again and again to different groups.

The ultimate in high-tech aids is the computer-linked system, such as PowerPoint™, which operates with a special overhead projector. This gives you a visual display that can be quickly altered from the keyboard to display results of several "what if" scenarios in a variety of display modes. *But* you must operate this package smoothly and expertly, or the technology will overwhelm your message and derail your talk completely.

THE BASICS OF USING AV AIDS

Whatever level and type of audio-visual aids you decide to use, you must know how to use them, and you must have practiced their use, so that they blend smoothly with the flow of your talk. Here are a few things to remember:

- Use your AV aids, don't let them use you. Your AV aids, as well as your cue cards and any other support materials you use, must *remain* support materials. They are not the presentation – you are.

- Face your audience and keep eye contact as you bring up your visual or bring in your sound effect.

- Don't stand in front of your visuals (for slides or overheads, arrange to have the display screen mounted high enough that this won't be a problem). In general, stand to one side of the display, and use a pointer to indicate features you want to emphasize. For an overhead, you can lay a pen or pencil on the projector stage, with its point indicating the feature you want to highlight.

- Pause slightly in your talk when you change visuals. This gives your audience a chance to look at the new material. If you don't pause, they might well miss what you say next. You can also use this opportunity to take a full breath so that you can refuel for the next point you want to make.

- Make sure that you're comfortable using your AV aids. For example, stand to the side and use the pointer hand that seems more natural for you. Don't try to point awkwardly across your body. Try this out ahead of time.

- And don't panic if the AV portion of your presentation breaks down. Go ahead with your talk while the organizers work desperately to fix the equipment.

Quick guide to making good visuals

- Four bulleted points maximum per page for clarity
- Two text lines maximum per bullet (more text turns a visual into a reading test)
- Two graphical elements (pictures) maximum per page (editorial cartoons: one picture, one powerful idea)
- typeface large enough to be easily readable by the average person in the back row
- Two different typefaces maximum on a single visual
- different type sizes of the same typeface where it helps emphasize or clarify a point
- Sans-serif typefaces for large headlines, simple typeface for text

Quick guide to using AV aids

- Use only AV aids that *substantially* improve your presentation.
- Make basic visual aids your first choice – flip charts, black/white boards, overhead projector and transparencies, single 35 mm slide projector. These are the most straightforward and least liable to malfunction during your talk.
- Avoid medium and high-tech AV aids unless they enhance your presentation *significantly.*
- If you use any AV aid, make sure you are adept in its operation. Check it out before your speech, to make sure it's working properly.
- *Always* have a spare bulb handy for any projector you use.

CHAPTER SEVEN

Learning your lines

"He ceased, but left so pleasing on their ear his voice,
that listening still they seemed to hear."
– Homer

You've written your speech out and refined it. Now, you have to turn your written version into a smooth spoken presentation. Your written-out speech will always be too formal in style and tone if you simply read it. People tend to respond more favorably to a less formal, almost chatty tone when they're listening to someone talking. You want the people in your audience to feel that you're speaking directly to them; you don't want to sound like a textbook! So the problem is: How can you make your speech a little more listener-friendly? Here's one proven method.

Read through your written-out speech. You've thought about and thoroughly researched your subject. You've organized it into main and subpoints, and added fascinating details, examples and anecdotes to illustrate and support those points. You've written it out in your best, grammatically-correct prose. Now it's time to read your speech out loud. While you're doing this, pay particular attention to the way you've put your sentences together. Do they sound too stiff and formal? Are your written sentences long and convoluted? If so, some of your best points may be lost; people can absorb complicated and convoluted ideas when they're reading, but when they're listening to you explain an idea, the material has to be clear or you'll lose them. So you'll want to present your ideas in clear, easily assimilated bits. This means that you'll have to keep your sentences short and simple, and avoid cloaking your ideas in obscure words. Once you're satisfied with your new listener-friendly version, you're ready to go on to the next step.

Make cue cards. You want to talk confidently and fairly informally to your audience so that they see you as a poised speaker who is giving them an informative, but seemingly off-the-cuff talk. In all but the most formal situations, a memorized recitation or a straightforward reading of your speech from a written manuscript will be a disaster. Your audience will tune you out in a minute or two. What you need is a good set of cue cards, so that you can remind yourself what comes next. This makes you sound intriguingly spontaneous rather than wooden.

To create your set of cue cards, go back over your revised written-out talk, and print or type (Simple sans-serif, 18-point tends to work best) your main points on 3 x 5 inch (7½ cm x 12½ cm) file cards, one point per card. You may choose to note one or two subpoints under each main one. (Some people prefer smaller cue cards, about playing-card size [6 x 9 cm, or 2¼ x 3½ inch]. You can conceal these easily in your hand, but the information content per card is severely limited.) Use only a few key words, rather than complete sentences. This will leave plenty of room on each to print your points in easily readable block caps, or to type your cues in a large, legible typeface.

Make sure your cue cards are in order, and number them sequentially. Wherever you want to pause for emphasis, mark the desired pause, or alternatively, print in a short reminder to pause at a certain spot. (If it helps, you can even write in a suggested length for a dramatic pause.) At this point, you should also *code* your cards (use *, †, ✓ or similar easily recognizable characters) where you want to use AV aids, such as a chart, slide, audio or video clip. This will help you to integrate your AV aids smoothly into your talk for maximum impact and effectiveness. Now you're ready to check your set of cue cards for continuity.

Check cue cards for continuity and effective segués. Lay your cards out in sequence on a flat surface and taking your cues from them, try giving your speech. If you get stuck, refer to your written-out speech. Did one card segué logically into the next, or was there something missing that you needed? Were there any ideas missing in the middle of any of the cards? If so, make the necessary additions or corrections and try again. If you've managed to get your cue cards in good shape, your speech should sound fresh and smooth, as though you've just made it up.

Remember, your cue cards are just that – cues or hints to remind you what comes next in your speech. You have to know what's in your talk well enough that those hints on the cards will help you recall what's written down in complete sentences in your written-out speech. When your speech sounds spontaneous and makes sense, you're ready for the next step.

Memorize your opening and closing sentences. You must be very sure exactly what words you will use to start and finish your talk. Of course, you must know them so well that you can put lots of expression into delivering them, so that they *sound* spontaneous! Knowing exactly what you're going to say when you first open your mouth, and how you're going to say it, makes you sound confident, knowledgeable, and in charge. It helps to "hook" your audience, so that they sit up and turn into interested listeners. Then you keep them enthralled with your smooth, seemingly spontaneous speech, until you land them with your well thought-out, beautifully delivered closing sentence.

A *memorized* final sentence? Why? You want to leave your listeners feeling that they've learned something worthwhile. A well-turned sentence that pulls your whole talk together makes them think, "Wow, I know what this is all about, and it's great!" It also gives them a clear signal that it's "loud applause" time. You can't afford to fumble your grand finale.

Quick guide to learning your lines

- Read over your written talk.
- Make cue cards (main points as phrases).
- Bridge gaps between cards.
- Number cards.
- Mark pauses for emphasis.
- Code cards where you want to bring in AV aids or anecdotes.
- Practice speech using cue cards.
- Modify cards if necessary.
- Memorize opening and closing sentences.
- Practice delivering opening and closing sentences until they sound dynamic and "off-the-cuff."

CHAPTER EIGHT

Rehearsals

"There are tones of voice that mean more than words."
– Robert Frost

When you're preparing to give a talk, remember that over 90 percent of the impact of a speech comes from effective delivery. Studies have shown that the words themselves contribute only 7 percent to the effective communication of your ideas, while the remaining communication takes place 38 percent through sounds – how you use pauses, inflection, emphasis and clarity of speech – and 55 percent through your body language. So, if over one-third of the message you're trying to communicate fails or succeeds based on the *way* you speak – the nature of the sounds you make – then you have to pay careful attention to how you sound when you're speaking. Since over half of the success or failure in communicating depends on your *body language*, you also have to be very careful how you gesture, stand and move while you're talking. You have to be aware of any annoying or distracting physical mannerisms that may sidetrack your listeners' attention from your message.

In other words, you have to interest your audience, make them believe that you know what you're talking about and convince them that what you're telling them is true and that they should believe it.

How often have you heard people talking with the rising inflection at the end of each sentence that says "question mark"? They sound as though they're not sure how they really feel about what they've told you. Do you believe what they've said? Hardly! You're much more likely to believe the speaker who sounds sincere and convinced, whose words "ring true." That's why you must project conviction and sincerity when you deliver your message to your audience.

This doesn't mean that *style* – how you say it – is everything, and that content – the information you're trying to get across – means nothing. But research shows that you *must* present your information in an interesting, believable, dynamic way. This means having *full control* of your *voice* and your *body language*.

DEVELOPING AN EFFECTIVE DELIVERY STYLE

Many people don't know how to talk, move and gesture effectively when they speak to an audience. As a result, the good ideas that they are trying to pass on just don't get across. They need to learn effective verbal communication techniques. So, what techniques can you learn to make you an effective speaker, able to communicate your ideas easily and effectively to any audience?

The most important is voice control. You need to know how to control your voice, so that it effectively transfers all your well-prepared information to your listeners' ears, and from there into their minds.

When using your voice, you must be able to make intelligible, informative and interesting sounds. Remember: "The I's have it!" Only if your voice has these three "I" qualities will you grab and hold your audience's interest.

A speaking voice with these desirable qualities is a voice that is fully controlled. To control your voice, you first have to know how human speech is produced and shaped. This means looking at the physical side of breathing: how the air supply is controlled and how you make lungs, larynx, vocal cords, tongue, teeth and lips work together to produce intelligible speech.

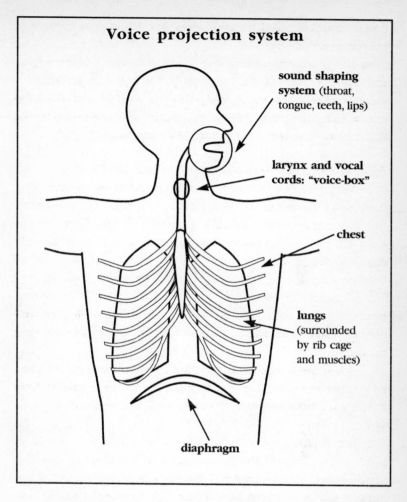

Voice projection system

sound shaping system (throat, tongue, teeth, lips)

larynx and vocal cords: "voice-box"

chest

lungs (surrounded by rib cage and muscles)

diaphragm

Just like an actor, a good public speaker uses the entire physical delivery system to project his or her voice.

Speech production and transmission flow chart

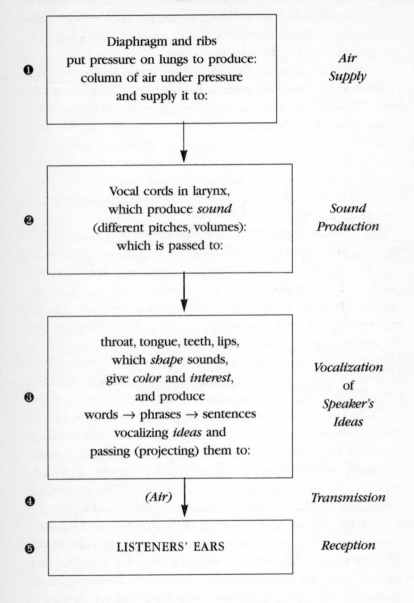

❶ Diaphragm and ribs
put pressure on lungs to produce:
column of air under pressure
and supply it to:

*Air
Supply*

❷ Vocal cords in larynx,
which produce *sound*
(different pitches, volumes):
which is passed to:

*Sound
Production*

❸ throat, tongue, teeth, lips,
which *shape* sounds,
give *color* and *interest*,
and produce
words → phrases → sentences
vocalizing *ideas* and
passing (projecting) them to:

*Vocalization
of
Speaker's
Ideas*

❹ *(Air)*

Transmission

❺ LISTENERS' EARS

Reception

The sketch shows how the body organs that help produce and project human speech are related physically. Starting at the bottom and working toward the top: the diaphragm, lungs and rib cage provide the air supply; the vocal cords in the larynx (or voice box) make the sound; the throat, tongue, teeth and lips shape the sound into recognizable words (which express ideas).

Let's look first at the foundation of the whole business of voice production: the breathing process. Just what is involved in breathing? It's mainly an involuntary process, meaning that you don't consciously decide to breathe (or not); most of the time it's automatic. You *do* have some control over the process, if you want, which is to say that you can force yourself to breathe deeply or shallowly, quickly or slowly. Many people breathe shallowly, from the upper chest. When they try to breathe deeply, they end up hyperventilating and feeling faint.

To speak effectively, you must take control of your breathing. For example, when you pause (for effect or emphasis) during your speech, you can unobtrusively take a lot of air into your lungs and fill them up by breathing in quickly *through your nose*. This gets the air right down to the bottom of your lungs in a hurry, like filling your car's gas tank right up to the top before a long trip. The air supply in your lungs is what powers the speech production machinery. Note that when you breathe in, or inhale, your ribs lift upward and outward, while your diaphragm (the elastic, muscular "floor" located just below your lowest rib, between your chest cavity and your abdomen) contracts and flattens downward, so that air rushes into the lungs, which are now free to expand to their elastic limit. When you exhale, or breathe out, your rib and diaphragm muscles relax, so that the ribs move down and in and the diaphragm returns to its natural upward arc or dome shape. This makes your chest cavity contract, so that it squeezes air out of your lungs.

If you practice, you can get a lot of air into your lungs in a hurry, and let it out very slowly, all under your conscious control. This will let you "support" your speech and control it, so that your audience can hear and understand you (essential if you're speaking without a mike). Thus, learning to control the way you breathe in and out is essential to speaking effectively. You must be able to control the movement of your diaphragm, because it squeezes the air supply right from the bottom. You want a continuous, well-controlled, long-lasting stream of air to pass through your vocal cords in your larynx to produce sounds that are shaped by your throat, hard palate, teeth, tongue and lips.

How do you project your voice so that the audience in all corners of the room can hear? You "squeeze" air though the rest of your voice-production system firmly with your diaphragm; faster for a louder sound, more slowly for a softer sound. Many people think that all you have to do to make your voice louder, so that it carries farther, is to *shout*. But shouting is done from your throat, without supporting your voice. If you do this for long , you'll quickly become hoarse, and if you persist you'll end up whispering with laryngitis!

DO YOU HAVE A PROJECTION PROBLEM?

How do you know whether you need to work on your voice projection? Try saying the following sentence out loud while you listen to yourself critically (or, even better, have someone whose judgement you trust listen to you): "To speak effectively, I need to learn and practice voice projection, by using my diaphragm to control my breath and support my voice."

How does your voice sound? A little thin? A bit wobbly? Too much like Donald Duck? If any one of these descriptions fits, you may find it difficult to make your voice firm, pleasingly resonant and loud enough to speak successfully to a group. You need to learn proper breathing and support techniques to help you project your voice so that everyone in the room can hear you.

So how can you check to see if you're in control of your diaphragm? Try this: Pick a comfortable place where you won't be disturbed, and stretch out on your back on the floor. Now, place one hand firmly on your abdomen, just below your navel, and talk out loud for a few minutes. You can count sheep, recite any poetry you know, say the alphabet forwards or backwards – anything that comes to mind, as long as you keep talking out loud. Meanwhile, check your hand to see whether it moves up and down as you inhale and exhale, as you breathe and talk. If your hand moves appreciably, you've filled your lungs enough to activate your diaphragm and your voice projection is probably fine. You'll be able to make yourself heard.

On the other hand, if it remains still or moves only slightly, you're breathing shallowly from your chest, not your diaphragm. In this case your voice won't carry to your listeners in an audience – you're not projecting. If you haven't room to lie down or anywhere private to practice, try this: Stand tall. Close your mouth, and breathe in deeply through your nose. Can you feel air moving down your windpipe, and your ribs moving out as your lungs fill with air? You should now feel a full strong column of air from your throat to your waist. This is what people in show business call "supporting" your voice. Often, it helps to close your eyes when you're practicing so that your surroundings don't distract you and keep you from concentrating on projecting your voice. Try the same thing again; only this time, after you've taken your deep breath in through your nose, let your breath out slowly and evenly through your mouth. If you're supporting properly, your voice will sound firm and steady. After you've repeated this a few times, and found that you can produce a firm, steady vocal delivery every time, try varying the volume and pitch of your voice to make your delivery more interesting, and to emphasize the parts of your opening sentence that should be stressed. Your voice should feel as though it's concentrated just behind your teeth.

Diaphragm exercises

- Breathe in deeply (through the nose) to fill your lungs quickly
- Force breath out slowly through the mouth, while saying:
  Explosive HO! … HO! … HO! … HO! (bounce off diaphragm)
- Repeat five or six times.
- Extend the number of HOs per breath as far as you can by working on the depth of breath you're able to take in.
- Repeat using FEE! … FIE! … FO! … FUM!
- Start again and repeat five or six times.

If your voice starts to feel as though it's dropped back into your throat (as though you've swallowed it), you've lost the air-column support that helps your voice project to your listeners. This will make your voice sound thin, weak, a bit breathy, if not actually quavery. You have to work to keep your voice supported by that column of air right from your diaphragm, and right forward in your mouth (just behind your teeth), but the results are worth the work. This voice projection, requiring full breathing and support from the diaphragm, is what opera singers use so that they can be heard throughout the opera house without using a microphone.

The breath and diaphragm control that you use to project your voice to your listeners' ears also allows you to "play" your voice as a horn player plays a horn, to give fine shadings to your voice, to add expression and interest to your speech. Even individual words can take on different meanings if you whisper rather than SHOUT them. So, you can give variety to your speech by using different levels of loudness as well as by varying the pitches of the sounds you make. Once you learn to do this easily, you can vary both pitch and loudness subtly, to give natural-sounding clarity and emphasis to your spoken ideas.

How do you know when you've mastered good vocal control, with proper breathing, support and projection? You'll learn how to recognize this as you practice the exercises outlined later in this chapter and as you get feedback from listeners in your rehearsals.

If you're a speaker, you're an athlete

To work well in public speaking, the human speech production system needs:

- conditioning
- toning
- warm-up

In other words, you have to get your muscles in shape and fully under your control if everything is to work together for delivery that's interesting, audible, intelligible and gets your ideas across to your listeners. So, you've got to be physically able to produce sounds that express your ideas well.

RELAXING YOUR BODY

You can't present well if you're tense. You need to be relaxed so that your body provides controlled support to your voice. If you are tense, your voice will rise in pitch, be produced in your throat and come out sounding like Donald Duck. So, how can you relax to speak powerfully and effectively? Practice the following techniques, and you'll soon lose that Donald Duck quack forever:

- Take five or six deep breaths (close your mouth and breath quickly in through your nose, to get the air deep into your lungs; then let it slowly out through your mouth).
- S-t-r-e-t-c-h, arms overhead, as you rise s-l-o-w-l-y up on your tip-toes.
- S-l-o-w-l-y come down, letting your arms come gently down to your sides and relax.
- S-t-r-e-t-c-h up again, then let the weight of your head and upper body pull your arms to dangle loosely in front of you, bringing your hands as close to the floor as you find comfortable.
- Straighten your back s-l-o-w-l-y, bringing your head erect last of all.
- Shake your hands and arms, and let them flop about loosely, for 15 to 20 seconds.
- Draw your shoulders up as close to your ears as you can, hold for a count of five, then let them slump. Repeat this manoeuvre five or six times.
- As you stand relaxed, feet slightly apart, arms relaxed by your sides, close your eyes and imagine that your head is pivoted on a balance point in the middle of your neck. Rock your head g-e-n-t-l-y forward and back on the imaginary pivot, decreasing the size of the nod gradually, until your head is still, balanced on the imaginary pivot. All this should take about 10 or 15 seconds and will leave you with very relaxed shoulder and neck muscles, if you do it g-e-n-t-l-y.
- Open your eyes, and go back to the first step. Repeat five times.

The preceding exercises are meant to relax your body, especially your shoulders and neck. They will also free up your breathing, so that you can speak easily, with full support, and PROJECT your voice, so that your audience can HEAR you!

WARMING UP YOUR VOICE

A baseball pitcher has to warm his arm up, so that he can make his pitch forcefully and effectively without injuring himself. You should warm your voice up before your talk, so that you can speak easily, forcefully and **effectively.** The pitcher does his physical exercises, calisthenics and stretching, even before he warms his arm up. You've done your stretching exercises already, so now try these exercises to warm your voice up and get into shape for talking to a group.

Vocal warm-ups Close your mouth, take a deep breath through your nose and tense your diaphragm to compress the air you've taken in. Now, pick a comfortable musical pitch and hum it softly. Then sing FEE, FI, FO, FUM, FEE softly, going up one tone at a time on each syllable until you get to FO, then down a tone on each of FUM and FEE, so that you're back where you started. Repeat this seven or eight times, singing a bit louder each time. See how many repetitions you can do on each breath you take, and try to do more each time you do this exercise! Now, do the same thing over again, but start a tone higher. Keep this up until FO is as high as you can comfortably sing. You can either stop at this point, and go on to the next warm-up exercise, or work your way back down again, dropping a tone at the start of each set of repetitions. In any case, do as many repetitions as you need to feel that your voice is warmed up, then continue with:

Lip, jaw and tongue looseners The famous Greek orator Demosthenes was said to have practiced speaking his words clearly while holding several small pebbles in his mouth. Although this is a bit extreme, you still need to practice speaking very clearly, so your listeners can understand every word.

First, your throat has to be relaxed before your lips, teeth and tongue can articulate words properly. The best throat relaxer is a yawn followed by a sighed "ohhhhhhhh." Repeat this one several times, until your throat feels unlocked.

Then it's time to limber up your lips, teeth and tongue. When practicing the following exercises, exaggerate your jaw movements so that when you come to do your actual speaking, it won't be a stretch but a relaxation. These exercises will tune up:

Lips: Relax your lips by putting them together and blowing, as though you were giving a "raspberry" or "Bronx cheer." You don't have to make the sound – just get your lips vibrating. If your lips don't vibrate easily, poke your cheeks with your index fingers and try it again. Now that your lip muscles are loosened up, practice saying "pop." Explode the "p" off your lips. Now try "bop." Say "pop, bop, pop, bop" over and over, until your lips are used to making a clear, explosive sound. Use that sound everytime you come across "p" or "b" in a word.

Jaw: Let your mouth drop open, so that your jaw hangs loose. Work your jaw up and down by closing and reopening your mouth rapidly 10 or 12 times. Now, wiggle your jaw from side to side a half-dozen times, while you keep your mouth wide open. If your jaw still feels tight, try another half-dozen wiggles. Finally, close your eyes and yawn! Feel good? Yawn again. Open your eyes and yawn some more. Your jaw should feel loose and relaxed by now.

Tongue: Say "blee-y-a-a-ah." Stick your tongue way out as you say it. Now, do it again. And four or five times more! Now, try saying "la-la-la-la." Repeat it several more times. Next, say "blee-y-ah-la-la-la-la" a few times. This loosens up your tongue and lip muscles.

By relaxing your throat and them limbering up your lips, jaw and tongue, you make possible the kind of crisp pronunciation that allows the audience to catch every word. These exercises will sharpen up your consonants: Say "t-t-t-t-t." Put your hand in front of your mouth. Can you feel little explosions of air as you say "t-t-t-t"? Then you are making clear, crisp t's. Now say "d-d-d-d-d-d." The puffs of air are not as forceful as when you say "t-t-t-t" but you should still feel them. Practice "dot-dot-dot-dot." Feel the air puffing out.

Using tongue twisters to improve articulation

Just by concentrating on exploding those d's and t's at the ends of words you can make your speech much clearer, but the other letters are important, too. Try some tongue twisters to sharpen up all your speech sounds. Say each one slowly, making every sound crisp and clear. Practice it faster and faster until you can say it clearly at a normal speaking rate.

Try these:

- Sister Susy slowly sews silken socks.
- Buy a bit of better butter.
- What about a wicker water bottle?
- Sipping cider, Sidney slowly slipped sideways.

HOW TO PUT MEANING INTO YOUR SPEECH

Once you've mastered proper breathing, support and voice projection and practiced articulating your words clearly, you're ready to look at the rest of the tools you need to get your words across effectively – to "sell" your message. A writer uses grammar and punctuation to give meaning and impact to the printed word. How can you get meaning and impact into your spoken words? The five principles you can use to make your spoken delivery dynamic and meaningful are:

- projection (they have to hear you!)
- pitch ("low and…)
- pace (…slow")
- punctuation (pause for clarity and meaning)
- perceptivity (look to audience for feedback)

Since you've already learned how to project and articulate clearly, let's go right to pitch and pace. "Low and slow" is what you should try for. If you're excited, your voice tends to rise, both in volume and tone. The breathing techniques you've mastered will rescue you here. The way you pitch your voice can enhance or detract from what you're saying, so keep the pitch of your voice firmly under control, and just a bit lower than in ordinary speech. This will keep you from sounding strident or shrill. You can then control pitch to lend variety and color, as well as vibrancy and conviction to your voice.

A loud, clear tone is important but you don't want to blare at your audience. Think of playing your voice as you would a musical instrument to put expression into the music. Think about the way musicians make their song louder, then softer. Think about how the melody moves from high notes to low notes. This variety keeps the listener listening. How are you going to get that variety into your speaking voice?

Use a variety of sentence types:

Questions force your voice to ride up and down. Try reading these questions out loud. Where does your voice naturally rise higher? Fall lower?

- "Why do gorillas live in trees? Let's find out."
- "Which part of your hand does the most work?"
- "Are human beings going the way of the dodo?"
- "Can we stop the earth from getting warmer and warmer?"

Statements contain important words that can be emphasized by letting your voice drop lower and by saying those words a little more loudly than the rest of the sentence. Try reading these statements out loud. Emphasize the italicized words.

- "So now we know that *many* extinct animals could have been saved."
- "*Some* raindrops are *five times* bigger than others."
- "Your *thumb* does more than *half* the work of the hand."
- "The ancient *Egyptians* made paper from the *papyrus* plant."

Try tape recording parts of your speech as you put expression into your voice. Listen to the results, and try again and again, until you and other observers agree that you've got it. Listening also to recordings of speakers like Winston Churchill will show you how pitch, pace and punctuation can make words come alive!

You can also use pacing, and pace variation, along with punctuation, both to clarify and enhance the meaning of your words. In normal conversation most of us speak quickly. Good public speakers slow down to let the audience catch what they are saying. One good way to slow yourself down is to put pauses before the important information in your sentences. Try reading these sentences out loud to get a sense of pacing:

- "Today I'm going to tell you about <pause> gorillas."
- "The wettest place on earth <pause> is Mount Waialeale in Hawaii."
- "How have we changed Earth's atmosphere? <pause> By cutting down forests <pause> and by releasing poisonous chemicals into the air.
- "Today we have many books to read <pause> because over 500 years ago <pause> a man named Gutenberg <pause> invented moveable type."

Not using pauses, or putting them in the wrong places can turn your meaning right around, so that you actually say the exact opposite of what you intended. The following sentence shows the effect of reciting or speaking your words without the necessary pauses. "Bill said Jane wasn't invited." Note the absence of pauses. What was intended was: "Bill," said Jane, "wasn't invited." Since this is written out, the necessary pauses are indicated by the commas. You would say it this way: Bill <pause> said Jane <pause> wasn't invited.

Now try it all together. Read this sentence out loud remembering to *pause* between important sections of your sentence and *emphasize* important words. "When *sunlight* <pause> enters a *raindrop* <pause> the light rays are *bent* <pause> and the colors *split apart* <pause> so that you can see each one." At first you might feel a little awkward remembering to pause and stress, pause and stress, but with practice you'll get the rhythm and flow of the sentence. Soon you'll be adding variety of tone and pacing to your speaking voice automatically.

CHAPTER NINE

Developing stage presence

"For whatever one has said well,
goes forth with a voice that never dies."
– Pindar

To talk effectively and convincingly, you have to practice putting your words and your delivery together before you face your listeners. You can't afford to appear awkward or uncertain in your movements and gestures either, if you're to convince your audience that you're an authority on your subject, telling them something that they should listen to. In other words, you have to eliminate distracting physical mannerisms – as the pros say, you have to have *stage presence.*

There's another good reason to rehearse. You need to say things out loud to find out how they sound; and you need to time your speech and pace your talk so that you don't race through it (a common problem if you are still a bit nervous in front of a crowd). You also need to practice using appropriate pauses for emphasis. After you've refined any sentences that don't roll off your tongue, you should time your speech several times. Then, add material if it's too short, or delete minor points if it's too long.

One more thing you should take into account when you're rehearsing – check to see that any AV aids (slides, charts, video or audio clips) integrate smoothly with your spoken words. While you're speaking, practice operating the projector or recorder, holding up charts, etc., so you won't fumble with them when you give your speech "for real," and destroy the impact of your message. If the audience is laughing at your comical juggling routine, the message you're sending out isn't the one you wanted to get across. If this practice with AV aids ends in disaster, practice separately with individual pieces of equipment until you can operate everything smoothly and reliably.

How many times should you rehearse your speech? Many professional speakers feel that a person can never be too well rehearsed, either on what you say (the _content_ of your speech), or on how you say it (the _delivery_ of your speech). You must practice *both* until you're absolutely sure of them. You need to be absolutely sure because, in spite of all your preparations, something is bound to go wrong during the actual talk. You need to be absolutely confident about every aspect of your speech, so you can rise above and cope with any unexpected hitches (the projector broke down, the P.A. system stopped working), and carry on effectively as though nothing unexpected had happened.

There are two essentials you have to practice until you're sure of them when you get in front of an audience:

1. **Content** You have to be absolutely sure what message you want to get across.

2. **Delivery** Your delivery style must be effective, which means that your voice must be audible, interesting and understandable; your posture and stance must be relaxed, alert and graceful; and your attitude and manner must be positive, enthusiastic and free of annoying mannerisms.

Avoiding that too-well-rehearsed sound

There is a definite danger that your speech could lose freshness and spontaneity, after many rehearsals, making you sound like a parrot reciting a too-well-learned lesson. To guard against this, memorize only your opening and closing sentences; rely on your cue cards for the rest. Try varying slightly the way you make your points each time you rehearse. As you do these variations, keep trying to improve the way you're saying things. Check the reactions of your "practice audience" as you go, and remember which improvements met with favorable responses. Then, add particularly effective words or short phrases (but not sentences) to your cue cards.

As you make these changes, your speech should steadily improve, rehearsal by rehearsal. You'll never get it perfect, but as long as your standards are higher than your final audience's expectations, they'll listen, and your speech will be successful.

PLANNING YOUR REHEARSAL SCHEDULE

In order to accomplish all these objectives, you need a plan, so you can rehearse effectively. You also need feedback from people whose opinions and judgement you value, on how you're doing at improving the areas where you're a bit weak.

Checking out your performance

To check out your body language and speech patterns:

* Rehearse, if possible, with someone videotaping your talk. Then, critique it with one or more companions whose opinions you value. (You'll be appalled the first time through, when you see and hear yourself.) "Do I *really* sound like that? Do I *really* wave my hands around?"

* If you can't videotape yourself, have someone whose judgement and opinions you respect watch and listen as you deliver your speech. The person should note any "tics" – but let you complete your rehearsal before commenting. Take the advice, and work on your problems.

* As a last resort, if you're on your own, make friends with a (full-length) mirror, and deliver your speech to it. This isn't nearly as satisfactory as getting feedback from critical observers, since having to be both performer and critic at the same time means you can't be unbiased. But, it's better than nothing and sometimes all that's available in a hotel room. Try to be as honest as possible about your efforts.

EVALUATING YOUR FIRST TRY

Use your first try at rehearsing your speech to check out your body language and your speech patterns. If the first attempt was videotaped, answer the following questions:

- Was the body language confident? Under control?
- Was the speech delivery well paced? Too fast, so that listeners couldn't follow? Too slow, so that listeners grew impatient? Were the words grouped in meaningful phrases? Separated effectively by pauses, where appropriate?
- Was natural eye contact established and maintained?

If videotaping was not possible, and the audience was "live," the same questions should be answered. While you're speaking, watch (and have one of the audience observe, as well), visible feedback clues from your listeners. Typical clues and their (probable) causes are:

- The presentation was too fast; the audience looked puzzled, then frustrated.
- The presentation was too slow; the audience became restless, bored, gazed at the ceiling, or fell asleep.

Once you know what and where the problems occurred in the first run-through, you're ready to start correcting them for your second try. To help your "live" listeners or those who are critiquing your performance on videotape come up with a more uniform and comprehensive evaluation of your performance, you should draw up a checklist like the rehearsal checklist shown. This can be used to give a detailed evaluation of your performance for all of the practice sessions from the very first to the final one before you actually present your speech to your intended audience. Be sure to tailor the actual checklist to your own requirements. Using a common evaluation list throughout will give you a fair assessment of your progress.

REHEARSAL CHECKLIST

| 1 | NEEDS A LOT OF IMPROVEMENT |

| 2 | NEEDS SOME WORK |

| 3 | OK AS IS |

Circle appropriate item, e.g., loud/soft – circle one.

1. VOICE

	1	2	3	COMMENTS
PITCH. . . . . . too high/low?				
LOUDNESS . . too loud/soft?				
STRESS . . . . in right places?				
PACE. . . . . . . too fast/slow?				
VARIETY. . . interesting/not?				
ARTICULATION . . clear/not?				

2. PLATFORM SKILLS

EYE CONTACT	1	2	3	COMMENTS
frequent/not?				
randomly distributed?				

STANCE AND POSTURE	1	2	3	COMMENTS
professional?				
appropriate?				

GESTURES	1	2	3	COMMENTS
natural?				
well-chosen?				

3. ATTITUDE AND APPEARANCE

ENTHUSIASM AND VITALITY	1	2	3	COMMENTS
genuine?				
infectious?				

POISE	1	2	3	COMMENTS
decisive?				
calm under pressure?				

APPEARANCE	1	2	3	COMMENTS
neat?				
appropriate?				

4. VOICE

	1	2	3	COMMENTS
appropriate for audience?				
appropriate for topic?				

ELIMINATING DISTRACTING MANNERISMS

The last thing you want to do is antagonize your audience, or distract them, so that your message gets lost. If you have body language or speech mannerisms that will annoy and divert watchers and listeners from what you're working so hard to get across (excessive, inappropriate hand and arm gestures, head nodding or wagging, or distracting speech idiosyncrasies such as "um, er, ah, like, you know"), work on getting rid of them!

After the first rehearsal session, take a good look at the videotape (or evaluations from your "live audience" critics), and see whether your gestures are choppy or excessive, your head movements distracting and unrelated to what you're saying, your movements about the stage uncoordinated and awkward. Keep a tally of your "ums, ers and ahs." You have to guard against these firmly, because the natural tendency of all speakers is to pause to phrase their next thought. Inexperienced speakers with fill the resulting dead air with sound – any sound.

Note any of these mannerisms that will disturb or distract your audience, and work on the worst ones first. Subsequent practice runs will be significantly better, showing a steady improvement as you work on the problems one by one. After a few more tries, compare the evaluations from your latest attempt with the results from your first rehearsal; the improvement will both amaze and please you!

When to begin rehearsals

Start planning your rehearsal schedule as soon as you know you'll be giving a speech. Of course, you have to write your speech first, so don't procrastinate! Decide on your topic and write your speech right away. You may change some of the details later, but at least you've overcome inertia and started. This also lets you begin actually rehearsing your speech well in advance of the time when you have to give it.

Starting as early as possible should give you ample time to evaluate (with the help of your constructively critical observers) your presentation strengths and weaknesses. This, in turn, will let you refine your presentation by "fixing" your mistakes in stages. You'll also get thoroughly familiar with the content of your speech. This is necessary; you need to tuck the material firmly into your memory, so that it becomes part of the "furniture of your mind."

What if you have to use a microphone?

Sometimes you have to use a microphone. In spite of the work you've done in developing your voice projection, the audience may be too large to fit into a room where you can make yourself heard. Or you'll have only a handful of people in your audience, but you'll be speaking in a school gymnasium or cafetorium where the acoustics are terrible.

Try to do some of your rehearsing with a microphone. You should rehearse, if possible, using the microphone and P.A. system in the auditorium where you'll be speaking. You will have to find out just how loudly you have to speak into the mike, and what the proper mouth-to-mike distance is for that particular system. You'll also have to practice maintaining that distance. With a lectern-mounted microphone, you can't move around too much or turn your head away as you speak. If you do, your voice will fade as you move from the microphone, and boom as you move closer. Above all, don't "swallow" the microphone. If you do, your voice will be loud enough, but your words won't be understandable.

For all these reasons, it's a good idea to practice your mike technique well beforehand. Some places will even have a clip-on wireless microphone, which will let you move around untethered by a trailing microphone cable. If you're working with a system that has a microphone cable, be careful as you do move, say to adjust a visual, not to trip over the cable or make popping sounds with the mike itself.

Applying the finishing touches – expression and eye contact

Some people, especially those who haven't had to speak in public, think that there's nothing more to a speech than the writing of it. They believe that they can stand behind a lectern, lean on it for support, read their speech – and people will listen. Those who know better practice the techniques you've read about in the previous chapter, so that they can be heard and understood, while interesting their audience.

But there's still more to talking effectively to an audience. People don't like to feel as though you're not really talking to them. If you stare fixedly at a point on the auditorium wall above the heads of those in the back row or, worse still, at the screen that displays the visuals or the blackboard behind you, your audience will feel that they're being ignored. You're not really talking *to* them. So, as you try to share your thoughts with your audience, make sure that you speak directly to them so that each person feels as though you're "one on one" with him or her alone.

How do you manage this? As you're talking, look, briefly but directly, at individual audience members. Say a few sentences to someone in the back row, then a few to someone at the side. Skip to the other side for a bit, then to the front. Even a brief glance and the occasional smile will convince all your listeners that you're talking directly to them – and keep them interested in listening. A look at the rehearsal checklists will tell you whether your audience thinks you established "natural" eye contact with individual audience members.

You should also rehearse using your cue cards so that you can refer to them unobtrusively, glancing back and forth between your cards and your audience adroitly. The same goes for the coded marks you put on the cards to remind you when an audio or video clip, a slide or a chart, should be coming into view. Practice reading those marks unobtrusively and producing the necessary illustration while you keep talking to your listeners, maintaining eye contact all the while.

Why do you need to rehearse?

Experienced public speakers are guided by an old saying: Sweat before your speech or sweat during it. Take your pick!

Rehearsing your speech

When?

Start as soon as you can.
Continue rehearsing.

How often?
As much as you can.

How much is too often?
You can never rehearse too much.

Won't it sound overrehearsed and insincere?

- Memorize only the first and last sentences.
- Use cue cards for the rest.
- Keep your approach fresh by polishing your sentences as you rehearse.
- Maintain your enthusiasm. Remember, you're improving each time.

CHAPTER TEN

Getting ready right before you speak

"Words mean more than what is set down on paper.
It takes the human voice to infuse them with deeper meaning."
– *Maya Angelou*

The day of your speech, you're going to be nervous. This is natural, but you have to get rid of the problems it causes: your body will tense, and your voice production mechanism won't work properly. You'll have neither voice nor body relaxed and under your control; your voice will be higher pitched than normal, your throat will close and your movements will tend to be uncoordinated and jerky. Obviously you can't afford to be nervous, but how do you get over it? The answer is to prepare both physically and psychologically.

WARMING UP

First, you prepare physically, using as many as possible of the techniques you've learned in chapter 8. If time is really limited, select two or three that work best for you. Don't forget to warm your voice up once you've relaxed your body and have your breathing under full control. If you prefer, you can use an integrated warm-up for both body and voice, while relaxing so that you can breathe and produce your voice without excessive strain or tension. You can vary the number of repeats according to your needs and the time available before you go on. In this connection, it's best to arrive far enough ahead of your scheduled speaking time that you can warm up for the length of time that you know from experience you need. Most people need 10 to 20 minutes.

Here is a successful integrated warm-up routine that many actors, singers, as well as public speakers use just before they go on. Done in sequence, these exercises will help you to overcome your natural nervousness, the familiar butterflies in the stomach, and allow you to focus on what you're going to say in a few minutes' time. They can be done before your final rehearsal sessions, as well as a few minutes before you "perform:"

- Close your mouth and take in a deep breath through your nose (this gets a deep breath straight to the bottom of your lungs). Hold for a count of five, then sigh it out quickly and forcefully through your mouth. As you give that sigh, let your shoulder, neck, and facial muscles sag and relax completely. Repeat a half-dozen times.

- Close your eyes and nod your head gently, fore and aft. Visualize it balanced on top of your neck, so that all your neck muscles can relax. Gradually decrease the amount of nod until your head is motionless, and perfectly balanced atop your neck. Enjoy the feeling of relaxation.

- Keeping your neck relaxed, stretch your arms horizontally out to the sides as far as you can, and gently rotate them in larger and larger circles. Reverse the rotation direction and feel your shoulders loosening up.

- Fold your arms across your chest and hug yourself by stretching your fingertips as far around to your back as you can. Now, rock first one shoulder, then the other, gently forward, to stretch arm and upper back muscles. Feel them pull, then relax!

- With your knees slightly bent, feet 10 inches apart, bend slowly and gently forward from the waist, letting the weight of your arms and upper body pull you down, and hang limply like a rag doll, for about 10 seconds. Then, roll s-l-o-w-l-y up to an upright position, starting from the hips, and straightening your spine progressively, until your head comes erect at the very end. Repeat this four times. Try closing your eyes as you do this one, and you can really savor the relaxed feeling by the time you've finished.

- Loosen up your lips, tongue and jaw by yawning hugely, and then relaxing. Do this several times.

- Warm up your articulation mechanism by reciting a couple of tongue twisters. Say "Quentin Quince, questing for quality, querulously quaffed copious quantities of quintessential quahogs," five times. Begin slowly, then gradually speed up, and change rhythm, volume and pitch constantly as you recite.

- Lie or sit down, hands relaxed by your sides; close your eyes and visualize yourself (in your mind's eye) in a safe, comfortable place, where you are completely free, with no worries or responsibilities. Pick your favorite spot. Relax in your imaginary comfort zone for several minutes, then take a final deep breath and release it as you open your eyes and return, relaxed and refreshed, to reality.

Now that you are relaxed and warmed up, it's time to prepare yourself psychologically. The biggest problem most people have to overcome before giving a successful speech, is fear of failure! The best way to combat this fear is to "psych yourself up," to send yourself messages that reinforce your belief in yourself and your ability to give a good talk.

Tell yourself: This will be a successful speech! I know what I'm talking about! I can get it across to them! Use these, or your own versions, as your "mantras" and you'll banish any thought of failure.

Not every situation allows for an extensive warm-up. If you are sitting at the head table or as part of the audience while others talk, you can still do surreptitious muscle tensing and relaxing to get yourself ready to stand up. As the time draws near for your part in the program, do a last-minute check:

- Keep yourself comfortable and relaxed. Blow your nose if you need to. Hum a bit to keep your voice warmed up.

- Make sure you have your cue cards either in hand or close by.

- Make sure you have water to sip. The organizers should already have placed a glass of water at the lectern for you, but don't take chances – bring your own! Giving a speech is thirsty work. An occasional sip (not a gulp) will keep your throat lubricated.

- Remind yourself not to twitch, sway, shuffle your feet, or drum on the lectern with your fingers. Such movements distract and annoy your audience as well as using up precious energy that would help you to deliver your speech effectively.

- Continue to enjoy your body relaxation as you walk to the podium or wherever you will deliver your speech. Keep focused on what you're going to say by repeating your (memorized) opening statement to yourself.

- When you're introduced, smile, take a deep breath and **GO FOR IT!**

 ## Quick checklist for achieving a natural presentation

☐ body relaxed, free of distracting mannerisms
☐ diaphragm and breathing under full control
 voice which is
    ☐ controlled
    ☐ powerful
    ☐ dynamic
    ☐ interesting, in pitch with volume, emphasis
    ☐ understandable, with clear enunciation
☐ pacing just right
☐ appropriate pauses
☐ an "I can do it" attitude, which telegraphs confidence

If you're nervous as you drive to the hall where you're going to speak, try some isometric exercises (tensing and relaxing shoulders, back and gluteals) at stoplights, to tone and loosen your muscles. As you drive, do some of the breathing exercises and lip, tongue and jaw looseners, in case you find yourself short of time before you have to give your speech.

Do's and don'ts before you speak

DO...

- Sip water to keep your throat lubricated.
- Keep two handkerchiefs handy – one for mopping sweat from your brow.
- Remember to relax physically and mentally.
- Be sure of your opening words.
- Check your appearance.
- Wear clothing that is neat and suitable.
- Think posture – no slouching.
- Concentrate on remembering not to fidget.
- Think positively: "I will be successful."

DON'T...

- Drink coffee, tea or alcohol.
- Eat foods that give you a headache.
- Eat unfamiliar foods just before your presentation.
- Get a fresh haircut or wear new clothes.
- Wear noisy jewelry.
- Undervalue yourself or your message.
- Worry so much.

Microphone preparation

1. Before your speech, check the sound system. Practice speaking into the microphone, with an observer listening from the back corners, center middle, and so on, to check that you can be heard and understood. Remember that a full house of human bodies damps sound down. Have your observer do a quick sound recheck in the back corners as you start talking, and readjust the sound system volume.

2. Check for proper mouth-to-microphone distance for best results and try to maintain it. If you suspect that you will probably forget, check the microphone sensitivity to change in your mouth-to-microphone distance, to see how severe the effect is.

3. Readjust microphone height if necessary before you start to speak. This is vital if you are 6'2" tall and the previous person to use the microphone was 5'1" tall.

4. Resist the tendency to "swallow" the microphone.

5. Remind yourself, as you begin to speak, that you're going to keep a constant distance from the microphone, and speak carefully into it even as you turn your head to look at various sections of the audience.

6. Check that your clothing or jewelry doesn't produce audible rustles, rattles, clinks, clangs as you move.

Mike talk

Microphone Style

1. Lectern-mounted

Tips for Using

- speaking distance –
  4 to 6 inches
- adjust height **before**
  starting speech
- don't turn head
  while speaking
  (this causes the voice
  to fade away.)

2. Hand-held standard`
   (Cardioid pattern)
   with long cable

- lets you walk around **but**
  check cable length
  beforehand
- don't wave the mike
  around as you move
  and speak
- don't trip over the cable

3. Lectern-mounted,
   feeding professional
   sound system, with
   control booth and audio
   technician

- speaking distance –
  4 to 6 inches
- audio technician in sound
  booth monitoring speech
- audio technician should
  adjust height **before** you
  start and compensate for
  reasonable speaking
  distance variations

4. Clip-on portable
   (Lavalier)

- two kinds
  - *wired* (Check your
    tether length and don't
    wander too far.)
  - *wireless*
- clip mike to lapel
- check sound quality with
  head in normal speaking
  position and adjust mike
  if necessary

CHAPTER ELEVEN

Impromptu talks

"No sinner is ever saved after the first
20 minutes of a sermon."
– *Mark Twain*

Speaking "off-the-cuff" is not desirable, but it's sometimes necessary. There are two main types of impromptu speeches; those that are self-imposed, and those that are brought upon on you. Let's look at a couple of examples:

First, consider the impromptu situation you can inadvertently bring on yourself. Say you're in a meeting, and several speakers have made statements you feel you really must challenge. You jump to your feet, open your mouth… and nothing comes out! You're speechless! This is a maximum panic situation. And it's hard to deal with once you're in it. Some people claim they can't tell you what they think, because they can't find the right words. Actually, they could find the right words if they had done a bit of thinking beforehand.

So, cheat a bit, and come prepared! Find out what's on the agenda. Are there any issues that might affect you, and that you want to comment on? If so, jot down your thoughts and organize them logically before you come to the meeting. Then read them aloud a couple of times, if possible to an "audience" of one or two people whose judgment you trust; failing that, to a friendly mirror. This will help to set them in your mind, so that you can state them with confidence and conviction when you stand up.

If, as the arguments start flying, you have an idea that you might want to jump up and dispute a point, try a bit of deep breathing as you sit (remember the hints in the previous chapter?) and hum (*silently*, *eyes closed* – as in meditation) to warm your vocal cords up a bit. Try also swallowing a few times and moving your tongue around, with your lips closed, to relax and lubricate your mouth and throat. All these should prepare you to speak dynamically and effectively, without your voice squeaking or cracking, when you jump up to make your point.

Here's a typical scenario for the second type of impromptu situation Someone you can't refuse asks you, on a few minutes' notice, to comment on some facet of your organization's performance; to introduce a speaker; to contribute your acerbic memories to a roast; or....

Be prepared! Always carry with you a small notebook and a couple of pens that work. In the few minutes before you get up to speak, you can organize your main points. (If you do it neatly, you've automatically made your cue cards. If you forget your notebook, make sure you have a few business cards with you. You can jot your points on the backs of these, and they make marvelous cue cards!) Then you can do the unobtrusive warm-up exercises mentioned above, and you're ready to speak when the big moment comes.

In an impromptu speech, you obviously don't have the lead time to make elaborate visuals or sound clips to spice up your talk. Not to worry! This type of speech is rarely long enough to really bore your listeners. But do speak well. Vary pacing, voice pitch and inflection, and presentation style as much as you can, without confusing your audience. If there are blackboard and chalk (white board and markers, flip chart and markers), use them to jot down a few main points as you come to them. Remember to say your main point to your audience, then turn and silently jot it down. Turn back and give details. Don't talk to the board!

Make sure your board work is neat, organized and legible, and that all letters and numbers are large enough that all of your audience can read them easily!

Semiformal talks (a.k.a. long impromptus)

There are many occasions that require a semiformal talk, about 20 to 30 minutes long, rather than a short impromptu lasting five or 10 minutes or a formal speech lasting anywhere up to an hour. Preparation time for most of these is normally from a few hours to several days, so that the techniques you use in getting ready are a blend of those for the long formal speech, and those for the quickie impromptu or off-the-cuff talk. The major advantage you have with these longer, semiformal impromptus is that you can sneak in a few more key ideas, and you have a bit of extra time to hone and refine your presentation.

Here are a few examples of different occasions that call for these semiformal talks:

* a farewell or retirement speech for a friend or colleague
* a congratulatory speech to a friend, colleague or employee at an anniversary, promotion, or award presentation
* a roast for a friend or colleague
* a toast at a wedding reception or birthday dinner
* a "how-to" talk to an interest group

If you don't grab, hold and inform your audience, you might just as well "save your breath to cool your porridge!"

TRAINING YOURSELF TO SPEAK IMPROMPTU

Finally, a few additional words of comfort: it's possible to practice doing impromptu speeches. In other words, you can train yourself to deliver off-the-cuff speeches, so that you become confident giving them, because you know just what you're doing! One caution: you have to practice frequently if you want to get comfortable as well as confident with this type of speech. Fortunately, you can organize short speeches as you ride the subway or bus, or walk in from the parking lot.

Impromptu speech - main features:

* short preparation time
* always carry pen and small notebook
* fast warm-up (isometrics, humming)
* short speech → 5 to 10 minutes
* few main points → 2 to 3 maximum
* timing: introduction → 1/2 to 1 minute
           main body → 2 to 3 points, 2 to 2½ minutes each
           conclusion → 1/2 to 1½ minutes

HOW TO PRACTICE FOR IMPROMPTUS

- Think clearly beforehand, so you know exactly what you think.

- Practice thinking clearly and organizing your thoughts on a number of diverse topics, until you find you can do it easily.

- Practice narrowing your topic down quickly. Impromptus are, by nature, short; you won't be able to solve all the world's problems in the time you have available.

- Identify the main point(s) you want to get across.

- Jot down the gist of each thought (in any order).

- Examine the list critically and number the ideas in logical sequence.

- Rewrite the list in its new order.

- Look again. Is the order really logical?

- Repeat as many times as necessary, until everything makes sense, and there are no gaps. Since this is an impromptu speech and thus time-limited, you may have to discard some of your thoughts so that your talk focuses sharply on a few essential ideas that you can get across in the short time you have.

- **Come up with a strong opening statement** that tells your audience what you're going to talk about.

- **Come up with a short, strong closing statement**, that firmly encapsulates your main point.

- **Say your speech aloud.** Tape yourself (audio or video), if possible. Did you stay on topic? Get your point(s) across? Finish strongly? Practice this whole process often until you're really comfortable doing it. After that, pick a topic and go right through the whole impromptu process every two or three days, to keep your skill level and confidence up.

Tips for everyday speaking

You've picked up on all the terrific pointers in this book, and used them in the speech you're preparing. Good news! You can use those tips to speak more effectively in everyday situations. Here's how:

1. Decide what you want to do: inform, explain, convince, entertain.

2. Pick from the techniques you've learned, to help organize your thoughts, so you know exactly what you want to say and can present your ideas effectively.

Some examples:

Informing

• everyone in your office when, where and how the year-end party will take place. Have a clear, logical, eye-catching poster ready, and hold it up at the strategic moment

• your family about all the details of the two-week all-expenses-paid trip for six to Paris and Vienna, that you've just won in your company's recreation association sweepstakes

Explaining

• how to set up and maintain an efficient backyard composter

• how to write a successful "how-to" book

• how to start and run a successful small business

Convincing

• your boss that you deserve a raise

• your co-workers to vote for you as their new union shop steward

• your friendly bank manager to lend you $25,000 to help you start your own small business

Entertaining

• friends with a great joke you've just heard (A lot of people really murder a joke because they only half-remember it, or they've forgotten just how the punchline goes.)

• seventeen children at your eight-year-old son's birthday party, because the clown phoned in sick late this morning

With a bit of planning, you can speak just as effectively in everyday situations as this book has prepared you to do in a formal speech.

Appendices

Additional information sources

If you want more instruction in public speaking skills, look in the Yellow Pages under *Public Speaking Instruction.*

Some boards of education offer public speaking courses in nigbt school at a nominal cost.

If you want additional practice, consider joining an organization like *Toastmasters International.* Contact them at 1-800-993-7732.

Useful references for speakers

And I Quote: The Definitive Collection of Quotes, Sayings and Jokes for the Contemporary Speechmaker, by Ashton Applewhite, William R. Evans III and Andrew Fotheringham, St. Martin's Press, 1992.

Bartlett's Familiar Quotations, Little, Brown, 1980.

Roasts & Toasts, Snappy One-Liners for Every Occasion, by Gene Perret and Terry Perret Martin, Sterling, 1997.

The Public Speaker's Treasure Chest, by H.V. Prochnow and and H.V. Prochnow Jr., Harper & Row, 1986.

A Treasury of Humorous Quotations, by H.V. Prochnow and H.V. Prochnow Jr., Harper & Row, 1969.

Roget's College Thesaurus, World Publishing, 1962.

GETTING ORGANIZED CHECKLIST

The first step along the road to effective speech making is understanding what is expected. Begin your preparations by making a list of the knowns in this particular situation.

1.   Audience size   _____

2.   Room size   _____

3.   Microphone   Needed?   Yes _____ No _____

                        Available?   Yes _____ No _____

                        Type available: _____

4.   Audio-visual aids needed?   Yes _____ No _____

      Details: _____

      _____

      _____

                        Available?   Yes _____ No _____

      Details: _____

      _____

      _____

5.   Speech length _____

6.   Topic _____

      Emphasis: explain? _____   convince? _____

                        inform? _____   entertain? _____

Sample speech

(approximately 7 minutes)
Type of Speech: Persuasive
Title: *"Drive Safely!"*

Introduction

The introduction stimulates audience interest and introduces the topic.

Why should we all try to drive more intelligently, more carefully, and thus more safely? In this country, since the automobile was invented, over 200,000 Canadians have been killed in automobile accidents – almost twice as many as died in action in the Boer War, World Wars I and II and the Korean War combined.

If you're using slides, show one with each introductory paragraph.

Traffic safety experts agree that if drivers were as concerned about this slaughter in traffic accidents on our highways as they are about people dying in wars, they would drive much more carefully, and the death toll on our roads would decrease dramatically.

So, we have a problem, and it's up to each and every one of us as drivers, whether on our city streets or on our highways and super-highways, to do our bit in reducing this horrendous death toll by being alert, and driving more carefully and safely.

Body

Traffic analysts tell us that even if we keep the same number of cars per person that we have now, our traffic death toll will only get worse as our population increases. To compound this problem we seem unable – or unwilling – to curb our love affair with the automobile. We are keeping our old cars longer, at the same time as we are buying ever-increasing numbers of new ones. Thus both the number

Pause before and after "or unwilling" to emphasize this point.

83

of cars per capita and the total number of cars in the country are increasing at an alarming rate. This compounding of the number of cars on our roads will inevitably produce a great increase in traffic congestion.

So, just how does increasing traffic congestion cause more accidents on our roads and what actions can we take to not only keep the resulting death toll from skyrocketing, but actually reduce it? Let's look realistically at the problem – in future we'll see many more cars and trucks in poor condition on our roads. Recall how the incidence of mechanically unsafe trucks and the consequent deaths from free-flying truck tires, as gruesomely documented in both print and electronic media, have shot up within the last two years – from one or two per year to *several dozen* per year. Inadequacies in driver training should also be of major concern. We seem to have a greater number of poor drivers on our roads, and we need to address this problem right away. In addition, the civility and trust we used to count on from our fellow drivers (and gave in return) seems to have broken down. We are collectively not nearly as polite or cooperative on the roads as we used to be – in fact these laudable qualities seem to have been replaced by a worrisome impatience and a dangerous intolerance of others' rights to be on the road. As a result of both these factors, many drivers – *even "good" ones* – pay much less attention than they should to laws and traffic regulations meant to keep us all alive as we drive and attempt to share that road in safety.

Details and examples set out the problem you are dealing with.

Change the slide as you are about to comment on its content. For example, at this point you might show a picture of a car after a truck tire has hit the windshield.

Underline or italicize important points to remind yourself to use your tone of voice to place emphasis here.

Use pauses and vocal emphasis to make sure the audience gets the point.

Moreover, many people these days drive too fast for road conditions. Pressure mounts each year for higher speed limits on our highways, most notably our so-called "superhighways." New cars are advertised as having higher maximum speeds, and the joys of the open road are emphasized in TV commercials. But, we don't have any "open roads" in densely populated areas of our country anymore. In our fast-paced, even frantic, society, with its inexorable time pressures, and our increasingly complex lives, drivers feel harried, and compelled to rush everywhere at high speeds, even if this means compromising their own safety and that of others because of their resultant unsafe driving.

The average driver acting alone doesn't have the capacity to control these excessive driving speeds. Many motorists, in fact, comment that if they stuck strictly to posted speed limits, they'd be "run over" by the rest of the traffic! Meanwhile, the slaughter continues, especially on long holiday weekends, when everyone is rushing to "get away from the rat-race." Organizations such as the Canadian Automobile Association have analyzed accident deaths on long weekends, and traced the majority of them to "loss of control while travelling at excessive speeds." What this boils down to, when we look more closely, is that many drivers go into curves too fast, and generally drive too fast for specific weather and road conditions, for example, rain-slicked pavement, low visibility due to fog, etc.

Take a pause with each comma.

Use a number of examples to give a sense of the gravity of the problem. Slides can intensify the audiences feeling that this is a problem worth thinking about.

When you ask a rhetorical question, pause to let the audience readjust their thinking from problem mode to solution mode.

Take a pause with each comma.

Pauses for emphasis.

What is the solution? How can we help solve these problems, and save many needlessly lost lives? As I've said, individually we can do very little. We must act *together* to make a difference, to save lives. We must, *as a group*, drive more safely, more carefully – because safe driving depends on the actions of *each and every one of us, individually and collectively*! We must *all* resolve to obey traffic laws, to use *at all times* safety features such as seat belts, that are readily available to us. We can *all* be part of the solution by having our cars inspected regularly, and *keeping them in good repair*. Finally and most importantly, each of us can drive more safely and reduce accidents if we resolve to *slow down*. It's better to arrive a few minutes later – *alive* – than a few minutes earlier – in a box!

Conclusion

The conclusion should be a call to action. Leave your audience with something concrete to think about or to go out and do.

I urge you all, each and every one of you, as you drive home tonight from this meeting, to join with me in tackling this serious societal problem – to ponder carefully the points I've made, and apply them so that we can move from being part of the safety *problem* to becoming part of the *solution* – thus reducing the appalling slaughter on our streets and highways.

Goodnight, and *drive carefully!*

**For fifty years, Coles Notes have been helping
students get through high school and university.
New Coles Notes will help get you through the rest of life.**

Look for these NEW COLES NOTES!

GETTING ALONG IN ...

- French
- Spanish
- Italian
- German
- Russian

HOW-TO ...

- Write Effective Business Letters
- Write a Great Résumé
- Do A Great Job Interview
- Start Your Own Small Business
- Buy and Sell Your Home
- Plan Your Estate

YOUR GUIDE TO ...

- Basic Investing
- Mutual Funds
- Investing in Stocks
- Speed Reading
- Public Speaking
- Wine
- Effective Business Presentations

MOMS AND DADS' GUIDE TO ...

- Basketball for Kids
- Baseball for Kids
- Soccer for Kids
- Hockey for Kids
- Gymnastics for Kids
- Martial Arts for Kids
- Helping Your Child in Math
- Raising A Reader
- Your Child: The First Year
- Your Child: The Terrific Twos
- Your Child: Age Three and Four

HOW TO GET AN A IN ...

- Sequences & Series
- Trigonometry & Circle Geometry
- Senior Algebra with Logs & Exponents
- Permutations, Combinations & Probability
- Statistics & Data Analysis
- Calculus
- Senior Physics
- Senior English Essays
- School Projects & Presentations

**Coles Notes and New Coles Notes are available at the following
stores: Chapters • Coles • Smithbooks • Worlds Biggest Bookstore**